Robbins Burling has had firsthand experience with the peoples of Southeast Asia. Between 1954 and 1956 Dr. Burling studied the ethnology of the Garo tribe in Assam as a Ford Foundation fellow. In 1959-1960 he lectured at the University of Rangoon in Burma under the Fulbright program. Dr. Burling, who received his Ph.D. from Harvard University, is the author of *Rengsanggri: Family and Kinship in a Garo Village* and of *A Garo Grammar*. He is Associate Professor of Anthropology at the University of Michigan.

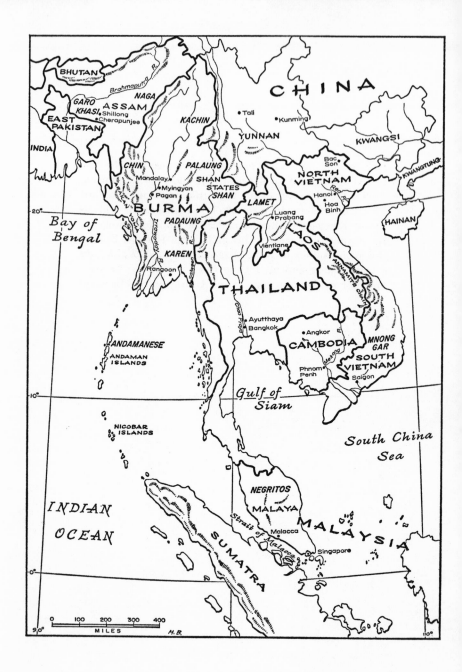

Hill Farms and Padi Fields

Life in Mainland Southeast Asia

Robbins Burling

Prentice-Hall, Inc. *Englewood Cliffs, N.J.*

A SPECTRUM BOOK

Preface

This book touches upon a range of time, space, and human variety far wider than that of which I can claim personal knowledge, but it seems reasonable for someone to try to draw together in a single place some of the strands of life in mainland Southeast Asia. Clearly, I am indebted to others for the bulk of the material included here, yet this is also a personal book, for I have not hesitated to emphasize the aspects of Southeast Asian life which interest me most. At the same time I have minimized or omitted aspects which others would consider more important. I have, for instance, slighted details of politics in favor of accounts of village life. I have tried to sort out the major foreign influences that have affected Southeast Asia, but I have given no systematic lists of kings, dynasties, or battles. I may have said more than some readers care to know about the tools and bones of the earliest men, but anyone who finds the details of prehistoric archaeology dull can skip lightly over part or all of chapters two and three without losing continuity. However, I have become so weary of overly schematic accounts of these early periods, particularly of the easy tendency to explain all early Southeast Asian developments by massive migrations, that I have felt compelled to summarize the meager bits of reliable evidence. In the remainder of the book I have sketched a few of the most important historical developments and described a few of Southeast Asia's many peoples. My hope is that the topics that interest me and have thereby found their way into this book will convey to others some impression of life on the mainland of Southeast Asia and of how it came to be the way it is.

Anyone who presumes to encompass such a range of subject matter owes more than the usual ritual thanks to those from whom he has learned and apologies to those who know much more than he. I have made two extended trips to Southeast Asia: two years of ethnographic investigation in the Garo Hills of Assam, India, as a fellow of the Ford Foundation, and a year in Burma as visiting lecturer at the University of Rangoon under the Fulbright Program. Both the Ford Foundation and the United States Educational Foundation in Burma have my gratitude for making my trips possible, as does the Center for Advanced Study in the Behavioral Sciences which granted me as a fellow the free time in which to complete the manuscript. A few of the scholars from whom I have tried to learn are listed in the bibliography. My debt to them is enormous. My parents read this book in manuscript and, pretending to be only "intelligent laymen," suggested ways of clarifying the story. My wife Sibyl and my children have shared my trips abroad and endured with good grace the ensuing disruptions to our lives. To my many Southeast Asian friends I have no way to adequately express my thanks. I can only hope they will not find in this book too much distortion of their heritage and their way of life.

R.B.

Contents

Hill Farms and Padi Fields

Life in Mainland Southeast Asia

Chapter One

Hills and Plains

Unity and Diversity: The Paradox

The corner of Asia that lies east of India and south of China is characterized more by its diversity than by its geographic or cultural uniformity. The towering mountains of the north have provided refuge for hundreds of distinct tribes and have slowed, though never stopped, the southward drift of people and ideas from China. Closer to the oceans, lowland plains formed by the great Southeast Asian rivers have allowed a relatively free movement of people and an easier exchange of ideas among them.

This topographical diversity is matched by cultural diversity. In the group of islands just below the southeastern tip of Burma are the Andamanese, who are counted among the world's most primitive people. They know nothing of agriculture and support themselves by hunting and fishing. By contrast, the people of the mainland river valleys are heirs to an ancient civilization which stretches back almost two thousand years. The Burmese, the Thai, the Cambodians, and the Vietnamese all possess long traditions of literature and art. The ancestors of the Cambodians started to build their monumental capital of Angkor Wat more than a thousand years ago and every region has a history of centralized monarchy which stretches back even further. Religious diversity in Southeast Asia is so broad that most of the world's great religions are well represented there. The people of lowland Burma, Thailand, Laos, and Cambodia are mostly Buddhists of the southern, or Theravada, school; the Vietnamese adhere to the northern, or Mahayana, school. Just to the east, in Assam, most of the people are Hindu, and those to the south, in Malaya, are Muslim. Even Christianity has a foothold which is several centuries old. Yet in the hills, many of the people have not yet joined any of these world-wide religions, but have remained faithful only to their tribal gods.

Today all the territory has been apportioned among nations which recognize tolerably well-defined boundaries, but not long ago this same area was marked by countless small tribes or even single villages which kept themselves more or less independent and maintained a fairly continuous state of mutual hostility or even warfare —a state of political fragmentation unequalled elsewhere in Asia. Hundreds of tribes considered themselves to be separate, distinct, and eternally independent from all others and the tribal map of Southeast Asia resembles the work of a wild man who has splattered his colors at random. Only a few decades ago many of the people in the hills were still enthusiastic headhunters. Linguistically, too, Southeast Asia is one of the world's most heterogeneous regions. It has hundreds of languages in a half-dozen unrelated families.

Nevertheless, to note the diversity of Southeast Asia is to tell only half the story, for beneath the diversity run numerous common threads. Among them are aspects of family organization, a respected position for women, the propitiation of malignant spirits, and similar technological habits.

Europeans are often surprised by the freedom of Southeast Asian women. Throughout this area, women do much of the marketing, join freely in conversation with strangers, and usually take a vigorous part in all family decisions. They help manage the household budget and, it has been charged, they not infrequently manage their husbands as well. This sort of behavior is common enough among women in Europe or America, but it is remarkably unlike the behavior considered proper in either China or India, which are so much nearer to Southeast Asia. Southeast Asian women are far more likely to share in inherited wealth than are women in China or India where, except for the dowries set aside for daughters, everything is usually divided among the sons. Furthermore, Southeast Asians less often organize themselves into large kinship groups such as clans, and the small families of parents and children are usually relatively free of domination by grandparents. In all these features the typical Southeast Asian family seems more like the European family than that of most of Asia.

For reasons that are far from clear, Southeast Asians have usually avoided breeding populations as dense as those of their neighbors. In Cambodia only a quarter of the arable land is even cultivated, and although the other countries in the area are not quite so land-rich, few people have gone hungry. To Europeans Southeast Asia may seem poor, but to the Chinese and Indians it has always seemed wealthy and open, a land of beckoning opportunity for their excess poor.

Nearly everyone in Southeast Asia worries about spirits of one sort or another—spirits who live in trees, who lurk on roads, or who hide in streams. Because the spirits are usually believed to have nothing but ill will toward men, ceremonies must be designed to control them or to drive them away and to assure the peace and health of the people. Many of the people in Southeast Asia are members of some more systematic religious tradition, but they are rarely troubled by the notion that their belief in spirits might conflict with their faith in other religious doctrines.

The staple food everywhere in Southeast Asia is rice, and it forms the basis of every proper meal. Side dishes often consist of some form of fish, though they may include vegetables or meat as well. These side dishes are called *curries* by Europeans, and they are usually so highly spiced with chili peppers as to startle the Western palate. Noodles are also popular, though more often as a snack than as the foundation for a main meal, and some people relish soup. The result is a cuisine that is something of a cross between that of China and that of India. Except where Chinese influence has been strong enough to introduce chopsticks, food is traditionally eaten with the fingers of the right hand.

Many Southeast Asians perch their houses upon stilts. It is pleasanter to be several feet above the ground: when the monsoon makes the ground damp and muddy, it is drier; in the hot season it is cooler. If the house is built high enough, the space beneath the living quarters can be used for storing household objects and crops and even for sheltering animals. The houses, always rectangular although their proportions vary, may be constructed either of bamboo or of wood. Whether the roofs are made of the traditional thatch or of the more modern sheets of corrugated iron, they must be designed to carry away the rain which is so abundant in most of Southeast Asia.

Iron has been used throughout Southeast Asia for many hundreds of years. In most villages there have been some who knew how to work it into their favorite shapes for tools and weapons, even though they had to purchase the metal from traders. Iron is so essential to the kind of life the people have worked out for themselves that it is difficult to imagine how they could ever have survived without it. Iron tools are needed to clear the forests for agriculture, and they must be used to work bamboo into the hundreds of objects essential to daily life. It is hard to imagine how the beautiful bamboo baskets that nearly everyone makes and uses today could have been produced without iron knives.

Other widespread traits have less intrinsic importance, but collectively they provide a unifying element. In many places women are "roasted" by the fire after childbirth to speed their recovery. In the hills, people adorn themselves with silver necklaces, bracelets, and earrings. Cloth turbans are often tied on in such a way that the crown of the head is left uncovered. Most of the languages are tonal and usually use the syllable as an important grammatical and semantic building block.

The prevalence of these traits gives an impression of unity lying beneath the diversity of Southeast Asia. But, paradoxically, it is one aspect of the area's very diversity that provides the most important unifying theme: each country in Southeast Asia has both hill people and plains people, and the contrast—and sometimes conflict—between the two ways of life can provide a theme which helps to bring order into our understanding of the area. Each of the modern nations of Southeast Asia includes a nucleus of plains people who form, in each case, a relatively homogeneous and dense population. Each of these peoples speaks a single dominant language, and is characterized by adherence to one of the world's great religions and subsistence based upon intensive "wet rice" agriculture. But each of the countries also includes a minority of hill people, who are always far more heterogeneous. They speak a multitude of languages, have had no political unity among themselves, and until the last century have never had more than tenuous political ties with the plains. The hill people usually practice shifting agriculture, and have been much slower to become Buddhists, Hindus, or Muslims than have their neighbors on the plains.

In spite of their proximity and the considerable similarity in their fundamental outlook upon life, the hill people and the plains people have met more often in violence than in love. As far as can be judged from the meager historical records, it seems likely that the contrast between these two fundamentally different styles of Southeast Asian life goes back some two thousand years or more. It may seem remarkable that these distinctions could have survived the blurring effects of countless wars, migrations, and the rise and fall of dynasties. The only possible explanation is that the differences in topography have limited the possibilities for development in the two areas, and have made it difficult for either hill man or plains man to conquer the territory of the other or to impose his way of life upon his neighbor. Hill people seem to have conquered plains districts occasionally, but in the process they have themselves taken on all the cultural traits which are associated with life on the plains. No doubt, plains people have also invaded the hills from time to time, but in doing so they have lost their plains characteristics and have been converted to hill men.

The topographical contrast is striking. In Southeast Asia hills typically rise abruptly from plains like rugged islands from a smooth sea. The plains usually lie at very low elevation even when hundreds of miles away from the seacoast, and they are always covered by a network of meandering rivers that facilitate the movement of ideas and people. This encourages the fusing of customs into a uniform pattern among the people who happen to live there. Wet rice is generally easily grown on the plains, and this can support a dense population. Relative density of population and ease of communication permit political unity, for armies can be raised and transported to conquer new territory and incorporate it into large political aggregates and this in turn allows a still easier exchange of ideas. The Southeast Asian royal courts, with their relative wealth and leisure, brought people together from all over the kingdom and from the world beyond. Priests from India, ambassadors from China, and traders from all over the world brought glamor and sophistication to these courts, and their influence spread throughout the realm. In this way, religious ideas and legal codes, writing and scholarship spread over the plains, but rarely penetrated the hills.

Travel through the hills was more difficult, and the prevailing agricultural methods did not allow the population to become so dense. Armies from the plains might be sent into the hills on brief punitive expeditions, but they could not secure enough food to support a permanent occupation or enough wealth to justify it. As a result, the plains kingdoms could never permanently conquer the hills, and for similar reasons the various hill peoples could not conquer each other, though they certainly fought. Hill peoples raided the plains and each other to take heads or to avenge some earlier grievance, but their raids were rarely more than hit-and-run affairs involving at most a few dozen men, for the hill tribes were not large enough to recruit larger armies. Hill people might menace or even terrorize the plains, but they did not have the numbers to occupy the plains permanently.

The hills have encouraged local political independence, and this has given rise to greater variety in all aspects of life. In some hill districts, clothing varies so much that it seems to have been deliberately designed to be as distinctive as possible, so as to set each group off unmistakably from its neighbors. Languages, too, are far more varied in the hills than in the plains, and each tribe usually clings to its own unique form of speech. Kinship practices, agricultural techniques, and religious rituals differ from tribe to tribe.

There was no way of breaking down the distinction between hills and plains until modern technology put roads, trucks and cars, quinine, and guns at the disposal of the plains-based powers. Only then could rule from the plains be permanently extended into the hills. This has happened in the course of the last century, but it is so recent a phenomenon that the cultures of the hills and plains remain remarkably distinct. In most of the countries of Southeast Asia, the contrast is so sharp that it continues to be a source of political conflict.

But hill people and plains people have not been completely isolated from one another. They have taken many traits from each other, and most of the traits characteristic of Southeast Asia are as typical of the hills as of the plains. Certainly the area cannot be fully understood without considering both styles of life. However different they may seem, they are but variations on a single theme.

A different unifying theme has been recognized in the term *Indo-*

China, which once was used for all Southeast Asia. For at least two thousand years, the civilizations of India and of China have affected the way of life in Southeast Asia. It is usually assumed that the Mongoloid racial type of the present population is the result of the migration of large numbers of people from the north. A few Indian traders or priests have been settling in Southeast Asia at least since the first few centuries of the Christian era. In more recent times both Chinese and Indians have immigrated in larger numbers in search of wealth and opportunities not offered in their own crowded countries. Not only people but foreign ideas as well came into Southest Asia and were absorbed by the indigenous people. From India came a theory of royalty, a system of writing, an epic literature, and—most important of all—the religion of the Buddha. From China came technological skills, political theories, and—from time to time—political intervention. (Vietnam in particular owes much of its present culture to China.) Although these ideas and skills have been accepted, other aspects of the civilizations of their giant neighbors have been quietly turned down: the caste system of India, for instance, and the type of family organization found in both India and China. Southeast Asia has accepted more from the outside than it has given, but it has accepted selectively and, up to now, has escaped being absorbed by its neighbors.

Topography and Climate

Three mountain chains cross the mainland irregularly from north to south, untangling themselves from the confused mountain mass of south China and extending at gradually decreasing altitudes as far as the southern edge of the continent.

The westernmost chain, which divides India from Burma, begins at the eastern extension of the Himalayas in the north, forms the Naga hills, surrounds the Manipur valley, and descends into the line of hills in southwest Burma called the Arakan Yoma. Finally, it dips under the Bay of Bengal, but rises again briefly to form the Andaman and Nicobar islands, and then curves eastward to form the backbone of the islands of Sumatra and Java in Indonesia.

The central chain divides Burma from Thailand. In the north it widens out, merging with the mountain mass of the Burmese Shan states in which live Kachins, Shans, Karens, and other tribal

Hills and Plains

peoples. Farther south, this central chain descends toward and through the Malay peninsula.

The easternmost line of mountains, the Annamite chain, separates Vietnam on the east from Laos, Thailand, and Cambodia on the west. Like the others, this line of hills is occupied by dozens of distinct tribes.

Each of these three mountain chains has served as a cultural barrier, particularly those on the east and west. The chains separate and enclose four distinct lowland areas. In the northwest lies the valley of Assam, through which flows the Brahmaputra River. Because the valley has had much better communication with India than with the areas further east, it has absorbed much of the Indian culture. To the east of Assam is Burma, drained by the Salween and Irrawadi rivers, and the home of a succession of Mon kingdoms and a series of Burmese dynasties. The third and largest plains area is that drained by the Chao Praya, which flows through central Thailand, and the great Mekong River which divides Thailand from Laos and then flows through Cambodia and southern Vietnam to the sea. A line of low hills separates Cambodia from Thailand along much of their border, but this has been a relatively insignificant cultural barrier. Finally, east of the Annamite chain is the Red River valley which constitutes northern Vietnam, and the lowland areas along the shore of the South China Sea. This is the part of Southeast Asia where Chinese influence has been strongest.

Encircled by hills are a few smaller valleys where wet rice can be grown and where miniature outposts of plains civilization have arisen. One such area is the Manipur valley on the eastern border of India; others are found in the Shan states in Burma and in southern China. Even in the steeper hills a few people manage to raise wet rice by carving level terraces from their mountain slopes, but most must live by shifting cultivation, and their lives have been shaped accordingly.

Southeast Asia is the land of monsoons. Most of the mainland lies far enough north of the equator to have distinct seasons, but the seasonal change from wet to dry and back again is more striking than the change from hot to cold. When it is summer in the northern hemisphere, the air over the Asian continent grows hot at a faster rate than that over the surrounding oceans. As the warm air expands, it becomes lighter and rises. This in turn sucks in air from the surrounding sea. As a result, sometime in June each year, rain-soaked sea winds begin to move steadily inland.

People who have never experienced a monsoon often think of it as a depressing if not terrifying experience, and they are surprised to discover how pleasant the monsoon season can be. For one thing, the monsoon is preceded by the hottest and driest period of the year when the thermometer may hover at 100°F., or even higher, both day and night. The dust that rises in the almost total absence of rain coats the nostrils, obscures the vision, and carries the viruses which make the hot season an unhealthy time of year. The coming of the monsoon changes all this, for the rain usually lowers the temperature by fifteen or twenty degrees and clears the air of dust. Even more important, it brings the world to life again. In the dry season the land turns brown and barren, but with the coming of the rain, it becomes green and lush once more. In more temperate climates, it is the warming weather of spring that brings the rebirth of life; in Southeast Asia it is the wetter and cooler weather of the monsoon that forms the closest equivalent. Only rarely does the rain fall for long unbroken periods. More often it beats down heavily for an hour or two but then the clouds break up and the sun may even come out, but it is likely to rain a little almost every day.

Naturally the agricultural cycle is determined by the rains. In the dry season, river levels drop so even irrigation is difficult. Crops may be planted somewhat before the monsoon begins, but if so they are planted in anticipation of the rains. Because plant growth continues after the rains pass, it is possible to raise crops which require very long growing seasons. But everywhere in Southeast Asia the heaviest agricultural labor coincides with the rains. Farmers may work in their fields while rain is actually falling, for to fall behind during the growing season can bring a failure of the crops and a hungry year.

The rains continue until September or October, when they taper off and the "cold" season sets in. To the Westerner and native alike, this is the loveliest of seasons. Though the temperature varies with the altitude and latitude, the cold is rarely severe, and the days are usually sparkling and clear, with neither the dust and oppressive heat of the hot season, nor the danger of rain of the monsoon. In February and March the weather gradually becomes warmer and drier until at last the monsoon once more brings its welcome relief. Southeast Asians recognize only three seasons: hot, wet, and cold. The four seasons of more temperate climates have nothing to do with the local weather.

Of course, no area as large as Southeast Asia can have a uniform climate. Where the altitude exceeds five thousand feet, ice forms at night during the cold season and in Yunan, a fair amount of snow falls; but most of the people of Southeast Asia never see snow or— except for hail—ice. Even more striking is the variability in rainfall caused by the pattern of mountains and valleys. As the monsoon winds sweep in from the sea, they are encouraged to dump their water wherever they rise over high land. This means that the coastal plains, and especially the seaward-facing mountain slopes receive the most rain, while the interior lowland areas lying in a rain shadow behind the mountains receive much less. As a result, rainfall varies from the world record of more than four hundred inches a year in the region of Cherapunjee south of Shillong in Assam to less than twenty-five inches near Myingyan, Burma, only three hundred miles to the southeast. And in the hot climate of Myingyan, twenty-five inches of rain accomplishes even less than it would in a more temperate region. These differences are reflected in the patterns of human settlement, for water is essential to agriculture, and only agriculture permits the accumulation of population.

The topography and climate of the area, together with the agricultural practices of the people, have encouraged rapid erosion. In some river basins erosion has been estimated to occur at about one hundred times the rate of European river basins. Southeast Asian rivers are always brown with mud; and the Mekong River, for instance, carries so much sediment that every year its delta grows some two hundred to two hundred fifty feet.

If the people did not clear their fields for cultivation, the climate and soil would support great forests. Many enormous trees are native to the region, most of them broad-leafed evergreens which shed their old leaves only after the new leaves have appeared. However, anything approximating a virgin forest is now rare. Great stretches of the plains are permanently turned to padi fields, and even in the hills land is seldom left unused long enough to allow more than a scrub forest to grow.

The unifying elements in Southeast Asia—the topography, the contrast between hills and plains, the historical influences from China and India—are characteristic not only of the mainland but of Malaysia, Indonesia, and the Philippines as well. For this reason the term *Southeast Asia* is often understood to include the islands. This book, however, concentrates on the mainland, and the term is therefore used in its more limited sense. This book is the story of the people who live in that area and of how they came to be the way they are. There are many gaps in our knowledge, for historical records are often incomplete, and even the customs of the modern people have been imperfectly recorded. But enough is known to sketch the outlines of their history and even of the area's prehistory and to suggest how the present civilization grew out of the past.

Chapter Two

The Earliest Men

The Evidence of Archaeology

Southeast Asia is hardly likely to have been man's original home, but men of some sort reached there several hundred thousand years ago, and their descendants—mixed with later immigrants —seem to have been living there ever since. The passing years have obliterated all but the most durable traces of the first men, so that very little is known about their appearance or their way of life, but enough evidence remains to leave no doubt that man's history in Southeast Asia is a long one.

The first men arrived during the Pleistocene period, the most recent million years of geological time, when glaciers repeatedly covered large parts of the earth. Of course Southeast Asia was too close to the equator ever to have been covered with glaciers, but it did pass through times of particularly heavy rainfall (pluvials) which are believed to have corresponded to the glacial advances in more northerly regions. This makes it possible to speak of four major pluvial periods in Southeast Asia and of three interpluvial periods during which there was less rainfall and the climate may have been even warmer than it is today.

Some of the earliest evidence of human life in Southeast Asia are stone tools, found in Burma, which are believed to date from the Second Pluvial period and which have been named Anyathian. The tools, though crude, are still recognizable as products of man's labor. Unlike the earliest tools in many other parts of the world, they are made, not of flint, but either of fossilized wood or of a kind of stone known as silicified tuff. Those made of fossilized wood are usually roughly pointed or oval in outline, and their makers shaped them only to the extent of removing a few flakes of stone from one side of the piece. The tools made of tuff are a bit more varied, but no less crude. Some are simply rounded stones flaked on one side to provide a rough cutting edge; others are flaked on both sides, resulting in a slightly more symmetrical tool.

It would be pleasing to have some way of determining what these objects were used for, but unfortunately no one can be certain. Archaeologists have bestowed names upon them—*hand adzes, choppers, chopping tools*—but these terms must be understood to be only convenient labels and cannot be taken as an indication of their use. Some of them may have been used for cutting wood or as spearheads, but the best guess is that they were used to cut meat. The men who made these tools were probably hunters. To catch anything but the smallest animal they would have needed some kind of missile—most likely a spear—but the tools that have been found hardly look refined enough to be accurately thrown. If spears or darts were used, they may well have been made of wood or bamboo. Both wood and bamboo have been used for these purposes even in modern times, and bamboo darts can be very effective—especially if dipped in poison.

Whatever their use, tools of this general form were not confined to Burma. Others have turned up in most of the countries of Southeast Asia, although they can rarely be accurately dated. Similar crude tools have been found farther away, in Java to the southeast and in northern China, and, like the Burmese tools, they are believed to date from the Middle Pleistocene period. If this estimate is accurate, it is easy to guess that similar tools found in other countries are about as old.

These objects differ strikingly from the hand axes and other, more elaborate, stone tools that were being produced in India, Africa, and Europe at about the same time. The most famous of these tools are the pointed or oval hand axes which, compared to the crude tools of contemporary Southeast Asia, are often symmetrical and delicately constructed. These carefully made Paleolithic tools never reached East or Southeast Asia: the line dividing the "hand-axe areas" from the rest of the prehistoric world is the oldest cultural boundary recognized, and it is tempting to wonder whether the division might not have been a reflection of biological differences between the peoples in the different regions. Only the very earliest tools found at a few sites in Africa compare in form and manufacturing skill with the tools found in Southeast Asia, and the African man of that period is believed to have been considerably less advanced physically than his successors. Conceivably, the early men of Africa and their somewhat later cousins in eastern Asia made crude tools because their feeble brains and clumsy hands were capable of nothing better.

Naturally, it would be interesting to know what these first Southeast Asians looked like. The question can only be answered indirectly, for no fossil remains of such early men have ever been found on the mainland; but both in Java and near Peking in northern China fossils have been found of men who lived at more or less the same time that the Southeast Asian tools were being made. In China, tools and human bones have been discovered in the same sites, and presumably the men whose bones are found can be credited with having made the tools. In Java, the association is not so close but there, too, the tools and bones may date from the same period. Actually, Java man and Peking man were much alike. Since the only convenient route between China and Java is across the mainland of Southeast Asia, similar people probably wandered there during the Middle Pleistocene period, and they could well have made the tools which have been found.

The early men of Java and Peking—*Pithecanthropus erectus* and *Sinanthropus pekinensis* were the names given them by their discoverers—averaged only five feet in height. This is a bit short by modern standards, but otherwise their bodies were indistinguishable from those of modern men. They walked fully erect, and they must have lived by hunting and by gathering wild plants and any small animals that they could catch with their hands.

The heads that surmounted these bodies were anything but modern. Java man, who predated Peking man, is estimated to have had a cranial capacity of between 775 and 900 cubic centimeters; that of Peking man ranged between 850 and 1300 cubic centimeters. Modern groups of men average between 1350 and 1450 cubic centimeters, so Peking man might have been able to live a normal life in the modern world—although of course crude brain size is not the only determinant of intelligence. Anybody with so small a brain as Java man, however, could hardly live normally by modern standards. He must have been slow-witted, and this is very likely the reason why the tools he left were so crudely made.

The skulls from Java—and, to a somewhat lesser extent, those from Peking—are characterized by a great horizontal ridge over the eyes. This brow ridge gives the skull an ape-like look which is emphasized by the low forehead (in the case of Java man, the head slopes back just above the eyes). The Java skulls look as though they had been flattened down from above; while modern skulls are especially wide and full at the top, these skulls are widest at the base. But although Java man's skull was small, his face was enormous and his jaw protruded far more than that of any man living today. He had a broad nose and little in the way of a chin, but his teeth were essentially human and entirely unlike those of the modern apes. All the bones in his skull were massive and rugged, far less delicate than those in the skull of modern man. The remains of Peking man show him to have been much like Java man, but his brain was larger, his brow ridges smaller, and his appearance in general more like that of modern man. This fits neatly with his date, for Peking man is believed to have lived in the Second Interglacial period, while the latest of the Java men lived in the preceding Second Pluvial.

One does not have to go to China to find evidence of the evolution of man, for the remains of *Pithecanthropus* are not the only early human bones found on Java. In fact, the island contains one of the most continuous series of human fossils to be found anywhere in the world. The series begins with the earliest *Pithecanthropus,* the so-called *Robustus,* who is thought to date from First Interpluvial. The *Pithecanthropus erectus* of Second Glacial is a little less archaic than *Robustus.* Then, parts of eleven skulls known as *Homo soloensis* (or "Solo man") have been retrieved from Upper Pleistocene. Their cranial capacity has been estimated to be about 1100 cubic centimeters, possibly enough to allow them to behave like modern men, and their brow ridges—though still large—are less impressive than those of *Pithecanthropus.* Still later are the two Wadjak skulls, which resemble those of the modern Australian aborigines, except that their brain size is enviable by any modern standards: 1550 and 1650 cubic centimeters, respectively.

Whoever surveys this sequence must wonder whether it represents the process of human evolution occurring locally on the island of Java, or succeeding waves of immigration. On the whole, the second answer seems the better one. The fact that human evolution in different parts of the world progressed along roughly parallel lines can only have meant that there was a continuous exchange of genes which repeatedly remixed the races and prevented them from becoming completely distinct. Because at any given period the more modern men were usually living somewhere else, the dominant trend of population and gene migration must have been toward Java rather than away from it. Nothing forces us to imagine that the changes required a great sequence of dramatic migrations, with each succeeding wave wiping out and replacing the earlier ones. More likely, a reasonably continuous drift of people eastward and southward during the Pleistocene period carried ever more modern genetic equipment. The new people probably mixed with the earlier inhabitants and modified the local population.

To anyone interested primarily in the mainland, it is regrettable that these fossils all come from the islands off the coast, but the same human types must have followed each other on the mainland as well. Coming from farther west, where human evolution seems to have progressed most rapidly, the people would have had to cross the mainland to reach the islands. The earliest immigrants may have brought with them the skills necessary to make the crude stone choppers and chopping tools that have been found, but those who learned to make the more highly developed hand axes may never have traveled so far east.

A gap in the evidence follows the earliest stone objects of the Middle Pleistocene, and only much later do human remains appear again. The fullest records for the later periods of Southeast Asian prehistory come from the nations that used to form French Indo-China—above all, from what is now North Vietnam. Here, starting in the early 1920's, French archaeologists carried out extensive investigations, and their findings soon became the standard against which archaeological remains from elsewhere in Southeast Asia have regularly been judged. The oldest Vietnamese remains were found between thirty and forty miles southwest of Hanoi and named *hoabinhian,* after the nearby town of Hoa Binh. Unfortunately, no accurate measurements of their age have been feasible. No one claims that the oldest of the northern Vietnamese tools can have been made before the end of the last pluvial, conceivably 10,-000 or so years ago, but even this is simply guesswork. The age of the various types of Vietnamese tools with respect to one another can be determined with slightly more confidence, according to their stratigraphic relationship and the more recent tools can hardly be more than a few thousand years old. If one were to judge only by the crudeness of the tools, he might be tempted to attribute considerable antiquity to the oldest ones, but as the development into more modern forms is reasonably direct and continuous, most scholars have surmised that even the oldest are to be dated in thousands —or, at the very most, tens of thousands—of years.

The tools that come from the lowest layers of the archaeological sites at Hoa Binh are also the coarsest and most massive. They are clumsily chipped pieces of stone—quite varied, but always irregular. They are chipped only at one end, and their edges are ragged. They do not appear to be much more regular or much better made than the choppers and chopping tools of Burma that are believed to be much older, but many mollusk shells and a few bones of elephants and rhinoceros are found with the hoabinhian tools, as they never are in the older deposits.

Many of the stone tools from the next (or middle) level are of the same type, but some are smaller, thinner, and lighter and appear both to have been made of more carefully chosen stone and to have been more skillfully worked. The men who produced them even seem to have made an attempt at symmetry. A few of the tools are neatly elliptical, and a very few are even ground smooth on one end. Most, however, are shaped only by chipping, often along only one side though some are chipped on both. More mollusk shells and mammal bones have been found with these tools.

The third and last layer at Hoa Binh includes more expertly made tools, although archaic types persist as well. The new innovations include smaller tools (two or three inches, as compared with the more usual six or seven inches of the earlier period). More of them are ground smooth on the working end, but none is ground over its entire surface. Somewhat surprisingly, bone tools are very scarce although bones of such wild animals as elephants and rhinoceros continue to be found. If bone tools were made during this period, they were not preserved. Since most of the hoabinhian sites are refuse piles or kitchen middens, consisting largely of discarded mollusk shells, bone tools should have been readily preserved if any had been dropped. The shells and the unworked bones do at least reveal something of the people's diet. They must have eaten plenty of shellfish, but they also knew how to hunt large animals. This most recent period at Hoa Binh also includes the first traces of pottery.

Rather similar tools have been found at a series of sites north of Hanoi. These are named *bacsonian* after the nearby village of Bac Son. The earliest remains there look rather like the middle-level objects from Hoa Binh. They are irregularly shaped chipped tools which needed little skill to manufacture, though a few have been found which are polished on one end. The later stone objects at the sites around Bac Son are much more carefully made. The trend was away from the more-or-less oval shapes toward more trapezoidal or triangular pieces. The cutting edges become more clearly defined and ground edges are more common. Added to the stone objects are a few bone awls and some ornamental shells. Some pottery appears for the first time, making the middle period at Bac Son similar, typologically, to the latest period at Hoa Binh.

Tools similar to those found at Hoa Binh and Bac Son have been found elsewhere in Southeast Asia and in Indonesia, but only rarely with enough associated material to give any clear idea of their date or of the way of life of the people who made them. In Malaya tools much like the hoabinhian have been found near the mouths of a number of caves. People seem to have lived in the caves and they certainly built middens of mollusk shells nearby. It is believed, because of the shells and the bones found among them, that these people had abundant river snails in their diet, as well as fish, turtles, wild pigs, deer, bear, monkeys, and various rodents. All the bones belong to animals that still live in the area, and this suggests that these people lived at no terribly ancient date—hardly more than a few thousand years ago. Many of the bones show clear indication of having been charred by fire.

Human skeletons have been found near Bac Son and in Laos and Malaya, some of them with tools of a more-or-less bacsonian form.

The bones are modern in type and show none of the archaic features of Java man or even of Solo man, but it remains somewhat uncertain just what kind of modern man they do represent. They have usually been assigned to some modern but exotic race: Australian aborigines, or the Papuans or Melanesians who live north and east of Australia, or even the Negritos who are still found in a few of the islands off the coast of Asia and on the Malay peninsula. In fact, they seem to have been referred, at one time or another, to almost every racial type except that which forms the bulk of the population of Southeast Asia today. The difficulty with these interpretations is not that they are unreasonable, but simply that the evidence on which they are based is shaky. It is difficult at best to judge the race of a man from his bones. It cannot be done with complete accuracy even with modern bones in a fresh and well-preserved state. The bones from Vietnam and Malaya are by no means perfectly preserved, and they have never been studied thoroughly enough to allow a confident judgment of their racial type.

To assess the significance of these bones, it is necessary to review the present racial composition of Southeast Asia and to understand the conjectures which have been made concerning the history of the area. Most Southeast Asians today are unmistakably Mongoloid. Their black and generally quite straight hair, their fairly prominent cheekbones and the occasional Mongoloid fold over the eyes make them resemble the Chinese. Southeast Asians, to be sure, are a bit darker and shorter than the people of southern China, but the southern Chinese also are a bit darker and shorter than their northern compatriots. Clearly, the closer to the equator one lives, the more useful it is to have a darkish skin. A few remote tribes of the Malay peninsula and the original inhabitants of the Andaman Islands off the south tip of Burma are quite different: they are true Negritos. They are short in stature (even the men rarely exceed five feet), their hair is woolly, their skin is darker than that of the people around them, and their facial features are not in the least Mongoloid. They look remarkably like the pygmies of tropical Africa, and those given to speculation can build wonderful theories of the migration of African pygmies to Asia or vice versa. Of course, it is also possible that similar jungle environments in Asia or Africa are conducive to selection in favor of this racial type, for all pygmies are jungle people. Whatever the explanation, the Negritos are certainly different from most of the people around them, and they remain something of a puzzle.

They are not unique, however, for there are individuals among many other populations in Southeast Asia who look at least vaguely Negritoid. Not all Southeast Asians have particularly strong Mongoloid features; some have rather wavy or even curly hair, some are quite dark brown in color, and most are quite short. When these characteristics are shuffled among a large population, an occasional individual is likely to turn up who looks rather Negritoid. A few Southeast Asians are also reminiscent of Australian aborigines. The natives of Australia are unique among modern people in their combination of physical traits: dark skin (though not as dark as that of Africans), plentiful body hair, heavy brow ridges, and protruding jaws. No population in Southeast Asia today can match them in all these traits, but an occasional individual approaches them.

Because of the existence of both Negritoid and Australoid types among the Southeast Asians, it is easy to imagine that the present population has been formed by the mixture of Mongoloid immigrants from the north who have mixed with and absorbed their Negritoid and Australoid predecessors. Some would also include a Melanesian ingredient like the dark and frizzy-haired people of New Guinea. It would certainly confirm this hypothesis to find human skeletons from several thousand years ago which were indeed more Melanesian or Australoid or Negritoid than are most of the people living today. The difficulty is that once one forms such an hypothesis, it is easy to find the skeletal traits to confirm it, but difficult to be fully objective. As of now, the suggestion that these early skeletons confirm the former existence of pygmies or some other racial type must be considered interesting but unproved.

Hunting and Gathering Tribes

The life of the earliest Southeast Asians can at best be only dimly perceived from the meager evidence of archaeology, but one other line of investigation may throw some light upon it: an examination of the most primitive people who live there now. We must be cautious in interpreting this evidence, for it is easy to fall into the trap of believing that modern primitives are the unchanged descendants of a much earlier population. We must also remember that no tribe is truly isolated from the influence of its neighbors. Of the people in or near Southeast Asia that are usually counted as most "primitive," the Malayan Negritos have certainly had centuries of contact with their neighbors, and they have surely borrowed traits from them. Because the Andaman Islanders live on lonely and remote islands, they are sometimes thought of as having been thoroughly isolated from the rest of the world. Yet their islands straddle the shipping lanes between India and almost every important port to the east. Indian and Chinese ships have been passing nearby, and occasionally taking on provisions or even being shipwrecked there for most of the last two thousand years. It is true that the islanders' fearful reputation among seafarers may have discouraged contact, but the reputation itself could not have arisen without some degree of contact. Thus not even the Andaman Islanders can be realistically considered to have been a completely isolated population or unspoiled relics of some earlier era. Of course, people change their ways even without contact and no modern population, however isolated, can be assumed to do things in the same way their ancient ancestors did. The point, then, is not that people such as the Andamanese or Malayan Negritos represent a direct survival of the earliest inhabitants of Southeast Asia, but rather that they have made adjustments to the same kind of environment and used technical skills rather similar to those available to much earlier peoples. It is possible that the adjustments they have made are in some ways parallel.

Few, if any, hunting and gathering peoples live on the mainland north of Malaya. In the 1930's a distinguished German anthropologist, Hugo Bernatzik, visited Southeast Asia determined to find the ultimate in primitive people, and he claimed success when he found the Phi Tong Luang, whom he imaginatively named "the spirits of the yellow leaves." They lived in the high mountains along the northern part of the border between Thailand and Laos. Unfortunately, Bernatzik made such incredible statements about these people that his account cannot be taken seriously. The Phi Tong Luang were said to have no personal names and to lack a pronoun for *I*, so that they could refer to themselves only by a kinship term (such as *the son* or *the brother,* depending on the speaker's relationship to the person being spoken to). Their mental level was said to be low: they hardly remembered the past or anticipated the future, and they were incapable of abstract thought. Their language was so backward that it lacked names for different species of plants or animals. The people were said to keep to themselves, avoiding contact with others; yet, mysteriously, they were able to speak Laotian as well as their own language. Apparently Professor Bernatzik let either his own theories or the racial theories popular in his homeland at that time prevent him from making an objective report. That is unfortunate, for if the Phi Tong Luang really exist it would be interesting to know something about them.

The Andamanese and Malayan Negritos are marginal to the area upon which this book focuses, but their environment is enough like that of the countries further north to make their way of life relevant. The Andamanese have long had the reputation of possessing one of the world's most primitive technologies. It has been claimed that at the time of their first contact with Europeans, they were the only people in all the world who lacked domesticated dogs. Although Negritos with similar physical characteristics are scattered from Africa to the Philippines, only the Andamanese have had any degree of independence within known history and only they have their own distinctive language. All the other pygmies maintain constant trading relations with their full-sized neighbors and speak the language of the people around them. Andamanese independence was maintained until the last century, when the British established an outpost of their Indian empire on the islands. The Andaman Islands have since been transferred to the jurisdiction of India, and India has recently been encouraging settlement from the mainland. The result is that the Andamanese are now a dwindling minority of their island's population.

When the Andamanese were independent, they seem to have divided themselves into more or less autonomous bands of thirty to fifty or more people. Each band claimed the right to exploit a territory a few miles in diameter. People knew about their immediate neighbors and met them occasionally, but of those who lived more than fifty miles away, they are said to have had no knowledge whatsoever. Each band had one permanent camp—a sort of headquarters to which it periodically returned—but it also had a number of more temporary campsites where it would stay for shorter periods. Because Andamanese technology never produced enough food to allow the bands to stay in one place, they were forced to shift residence periodically in order to have convenient access to new resources. The bands that lived near the coast used boats for their travels and could get around more easily than the inlanders, who had to walk. The inland people sometimes built communal huts as large as sixty feet in diameter. Other bands, especially those on the coast, built a circle of semipermanent huts, each of which was occupied by one family group. The hunting camps were occupied for shorter periods, and the huts built there were simpler and less permanent. A special hut seems always to have been set aside for the unmarried youths.

There was little division of labor among the Andamanese except between men and women, but here the division was clear. Men were first of all hunters. Each man made his own weapons and, in areas where boats were used, the men built them. Women contributed to the food supply by collecting the vegetables that grew wild in their country. Every member of the band had the right to use and exploit the resources of its territory, but almost everything else was owned by individuals. Even a tree could be reserved by the man who first saw it, and only he could make a canoe from it. Within the band, the family was the most important group. There was considerable sexual freedom before marriage, but adultery was frowned upon. There were few marriage restrictions, except that one could not marry a close kinsman. Children solidified marriage and made it more permanent. Husband and wife provided their different types of food for each other, and they cooked and ate in common.

Like the Andamanese, most of the Negritos of Malaya were hunters and gatherers. They were not mountaineers, but lived in the valleys or in the foothills of northern Malaya, often at no great distance from Malay settlements. The higher hills more often were occupied by shifting agriculturalists (the Senoi, who were not predominantly Negrito in race. However, Negritos sometimes planted a few crops to supplement their hunting, and the Senoi might also hunt, so the distinction in their way of life is by no means complete. Moreover, both Negritos and Senoi spoke languages which seem to be related, if only distantly, to the languages of historically important people: the Mon of Burma and the Khmer of modern Cambodia. This Mon-Khmer group of languages may have been in Southeast Asia as long as any other, but it cannot regularly be attributed to the most primitive peoples, and only in Malaya is it spoken by Negritos.

No more than a few thousand Negritos survive today, and most of them live on reservations under government protection, rather like many American Indians in the United States. Their original habitat was an area of extensive swamps, short rivers, and dense forests. They led an even more wandering life than the Andamanese, for they rarely stayed in one spot for more than three days before moving on to search for food. Like the Andamanese, they lived in independent bands. Six or seven families—a total of perhaps thirty people of all ages—cooperated with one another and jointly exploited a common territory, but individual men owned fruit trees (and Ipoh trees, from which poison was made), and this gave the family an important resource separate from their common right to the resources of the band. The band migrated as a unit, and neighboring bands are said to have lived in complete peace and to have allowed each other to wander over their territories so long as they did not molest the fruit trees. Toward non-Negritos, too, they are said to have been peaceful or even passive, for they would retire timidly into the forest rather than resist encroachment.

Their camps consisted of a number of family shelters facing inward around a rough oval. Sometimes the shelters were arranged in two parallel lines laid so close together that the path between them formed a virtual tunnel. Usually, the shelter was little more than a lean-to—a frame of three or four slanting posts and a slender ridgepole, covered with leaves. Inside the huts were bamboo sleeping platforms; in front or at the side the families built smoky fires which warmed them at night and also helped to drive away mosquitoes. If the need for more food had not driven the bands to move regularly, their accumulated rubbish probably would have, since it was tossed indiscriminately about the camp.

The men hunted, fished, gathered fruit and firewood, and made their own tools and weapons. The women were responsible for the domestic chores of child-tending and cooking, but they also made mats and baskets, did much of the work of building their shelters, and contributed an important part of the family food supply by digging for edible roots. Women enjoyed a status of near-equality with their husbands; it is said that they were never beaten or oppressed by the men. Polygyny was rare, but divorce was easy, and the Negritos changed their partners frequently at the initiative of either husband or wife.

Negrito technology was simple. Most of their manufactures were made from bamboo. They caught fish with various types of traps, rods and lines, spears, or even harpoons. They sometimes hunted with bamboo-tipped spears, but they also hunted with blowguns—delicate devices made from tubes of bamboo about seven feet long. A strong puff of breath through a blowgun could propel a poisoned dart twenty-five yards with considerable accuracy, and the poison was strong enough to kill a large animal, though the darts were more often used for small game. Instead of manufacturing these blowguns, the Negritos purchased them from other tribes, and for this reason it has been claimed that the blowgun was not a weapon native to them. Instead, the bow and arrow, has been considered their aboriginal weapon, although they often used iron-tipped arrows. Negritos have always traded with the neighboring Malays, selling them jungle products and obtaining in return metal articles, salt, beads, and cloth. It may be doubted whether even their rudimentary bamboo technology would have been possible without the use of metal knives.

The Negritos recognized many sorts of supernatural beings. They believed that animals as well as humans possessed souls. The ghosts of the dead might live happily in a spirit world, but they sometimes returned to haunt their graves. There were spirits of heavenly bodies and natural phenomena, and elf-like spirits that inhabited flowers. The Negritos had gods, too, though these required less ritual than the more petty but irritating spirits and ghosts. The most powerful deity was the god of thunder who, when angry, tossed his thunderbolts to warn or to punish men. Death and disease were attributed to witchcraft or to the malevolence of supernatural beings. It was believed that a man could magically injure his enemies, but he could also use charms and amulets to protect himself.

No people living in Southeast Asia today have a more primitive technology than the Andamanese or Malayan Negritos. A few generations ago these two groups lived much as people could have lived several thousand years ago. The natural forests are blessed with plentiful wild fruits and animals which would have provided ample food for a thin population of wandering hunters, but—except perhaps where shellfish were abundant—it was probably scarce enough to forbid a settled life in permanent villages. Division of population into small bands seems to be the most efficient way to exploit such resources. The available food might support a band of several families, but no more. A band could work most efficiently within a familiar territory. Spears, bows and arrows, fish traps, and blowguns are all useful for such a life and may be very ancient inventions, but too many possessions can only interfere with a wandering life. It is tempting to see the young men's houses of the Andamanese, the long list of Negrito spirits, the simple family structure and the relatively free position of the women in both groups as forerunners of the civilization that has developed in Southeast Asia, but other kinds of family organization or religion might have been just as feasible in that environment, and on the whole it is difficult to see an intimate link between these few scattered hunters and the agricultural people who so greatly outnumber them.

Intriguing as they are, hunting and gathering people are about as characteristic of Southeast Asia today as Algonquian Indians are typical of modern Manhattan. Almost everywhere, their way of life has long been replaced by agriculture. Just as it is misleading to imagine that the few remaining hunters are the direct heirs of the original inhabitants of Southeast Asia, so is it an oversimplification to imagine that all the other peoples, together with their more complex technology, simply migrated in from other parts of the world, all but wiping out the older autochthonous population. A popular view of Southeast Asian prehistory is that the ancestors of many of the modern peoples migrated southward from what is now China. Hopeful scholars have even tried to reconstruct several waves of immigrants, each of a distinctive racial type, and each with its characteristic tools and language. It has often been claimed that one or another modern tribe or people had its "origin" in some other place, and reached its present territory by migration. No doubt people have migrated (though it may be questioned whether all the migration has been from north to south as is so often imagined). No doubt ideas have come into Southeast Asia from other parts of the world. But people have continually mixed both culturally and genetically, and no group in Southeast Asia can claim a single, pure ancestry. Some of the traits of modern Southeast Asia have been found there for a very long time; others have come from China, from India, or from the West. To ask: "What is the origin of the Burmese?" as is so often done, is exactly like asking: "What is the origin of the French?" Like the French, the Burmese represent a modern synthesis of genetic and cultural elements which originated in many parts of the world but which joined together in their own unique way in Burma. The same thing is true of all the hundreds of ethnic groups in Southeast Asia.

The "origin" of the people of Southeast Asia, therefore, is not to be found by pointing to some remote spot on the map but by sifting out the many components of their civilization and trying to understand how each of them became established. What little historical evidence we have must be examined in an effort to determine which elements were imported from the outside and which developed locally. The stone tools of the early hunting peoples provide a hint of one of the oldest local traits, but it is one which has long been submerged under other elements. Of all the components of Southeast Asian civilization, none is more important than the methods of food production, and it is to the evidence for the beginnings of agriculture that we now turn.

Chapter Three

Agriculture

The Chief Crops and Animals

It is impossible to determine with assurance at what time or place—or even in what form—agriculture was first practiced in Southeast Asia. Nevertheless, agriculture brought such changes in man's life that the guesses that have been made must be considered and what little evidence exists must be weighed.

A number of scholars have believed that several plants and animals were first domesticated in Southeast Asia and that only later did they spread to other parts of the world. The botanist, Carl Sauer, even suggested that man's very first experiments with agriculture took place in Southeast Asia and that the idea of agriculture itself spread from there to the rest of the world. But as solid archaeological evidence testifies to about eight thousand years of agriculture in the Middle East and to hardly a quarter of that in Southeast Asia, this can perhaps be dismissed as a rather fanciful suggestion. Nevertheless, the evidence for the Southeast Asian origins of certain specific domestic plants is stronger, even if their first deliberate cultivation was much more recent than the original plant domestication in the Middle East. The wild forms of several domestic plants seem to be native to Southeast Asia and this implies that they were first domesticated there. Today, many of these plants are distributed throughout much of the tropical world, but this can be explained by man's having traded and carried away from their point of origin those which he found useful. Most of these plants are little known outside the tropics because they cannot grow without the heat and rain that their wild ancestors had become adapted to. Many are root crops, or tubers, with a high starch content and a meager supply of other nutritional requirements. Taro and yams, for instance, are satisfying staples but for a balanced diet they must

28

be supplemented with other foods—particularly a source of protein. Neither taro nor yams are cultivated from seeds, but from cuttings taken from a parent plant. The root stock is divided or a cutting may be taken from the stem or tuber. These will grow into full plants which can in turn be divided and redivided indefinitely. Several of the most important crops of Southeast Asia are propagated by cuttings. A number of scholars have felt this to be a somewhat simpler and more rudimentary agricultural technique than planting from seed and have argued from this for the great antiquity of Southeast Asian agriculture.

Bananas and plantains also seem to be native to the region and, like taro and yams, are normally propagated from cuttings. Although they grow on small trees rather than beneath the ground, they provide as starchy a diet as the tubers. In some parts of the world they form the staple crop, but in Southeast Asia today they are rarely used as more than a supplementary food. Breadfruit and the pith of the Sago palm—neither of which is much known out of the tropics—have a high starch yield and are used in a few places as staples. Ginger, also a tuber grown from cuttings, seems to be an ancient product of the region; it is used as a condiment rather than a staple. Sugar cane and citrus fruits—and perhaps the coconut as well—probably originated in Southeast Asia, though all have since spread widely over the earth.

By far the most important nonfood plant is bamboo. Although the shoots of bamboo are widely eaten, the most important use of the plants is in the manufacture of household goods. The people of Southeast Asia regularly use wild bamboo, but they also plant and cultivate the more highly valued varieties. Today Southeast Asians use bamboo for so many purposes that they find it difficult to imagine a country where bamboo does not grow, and it is tempting for an outsider to characterize the people as having "bamboo cultures." Houses are often built largely of bamboo. Heavy pieces serve as beams and joists. Walls and floors can be lined with matting of split bamboo, made by splitting the pole open on one side and then, in effect, unrolling it. The unrolled strips are then woven together to make mats. Finer strips can be woven into delicate baskets. Since bamboo is hollow except for the periodic interruption of the nodes, a short section with a node at one end makes a convenient container. Green sections can even be used as cooking pots, for the bamboo will char but not burn at first use. It can then be thrown away, for bamboo is so plentiful that another section can be easily cut when it's time to prepare the next meal. Dried bamboo burns too rapidly and gives off too much smoke for the best cooking fire, but it makes wonderful kindling and convenient torches.

Bark cloth is widely used in the tropics, and in Southeast Asia it may have been used for as long as the food crops. It is made by beating flat the inner bark of certain trees. The product is not so soft as woven cloth but it can be decorated and folded around the body in a somewhat similar manner.

Another crop, certainly the most important today, is sometimes attributed to Southeast Asia: rice. It has been generally assumed that rice was domesticated somewhat later than the crops already mentioned, though evidence for this assumption is anything but solid. Rice is grown by two sharply contrasting techniques. Whenever the land is flat enough and water so plentiful and manageable that it can be led to and away from the fields systematically, rice is grown under water. "Wet rice" is almost always planted first in a specially prepared seed bed where it grows until the seedlings are several inches tall. Meanwhile, the fields, or "padis," must be carefully prepared for the rice plants; they are thoroughly cleaned of weeds, and the soil is pulverized and soaked until it becomes a mire of heavy mud. Early in the rainy season, the seedlings are transplanted from the seed beds to the regular fields—one of the most laborious of jobs and certainly the dirtiest, for each individual seedling must be planted in the thick black mud. Men, women, and children usually all turn out together so as to finish the transplanting on time. Once the seedlings are transplanted, however, there is little more to do except to keep the dikes in repair and to regulate the flow of water, for during most of the growing season the padis must be covered by a few inches of water so that only the upper stalks and leaves of the rice plant can be seen waving above the surface. Shortly before the rice ripens, the water is drained from the fields, and about a month later the rice is harvested. Similar rice-growing techniques are used in India, China, and Japan, for wet rice forms the staple of most of the dense populations of Asia.

Where the terrain makes it difficult to construct fields flat enough to be flooded, Southeast Asians use a different technique for growing rice. The shifting or "slash-and-burn" agriculture of the hills requires a variety of rice that can thrive with the water obtained from rainfall and is not dependent upon flooding. The seeds of this "dry rice" are planted directly into the soil and the crop grows in much the same way as wheat or any of the other better known grains of temperate climates. The ground does not have to be so carefully prepared in advance, but new fields must be periodically cleared of trees and brush and, the problem of keeping down the weeds is much more difficult than in wet fields. Dry cultivation is hard on the soil, especially as those who practice it rarely make any attempt to fertilize. As a result, a year or two of dry cultivation depletes the land's fertility so that it is temporarily useless, and it must be abandoned for a few years while the forest is allowed to grow up again. After the land has regained its fertility, the forest can be cleared once more. It must be burned, and the crops are usually planted in the ashes of the fire. Hill farmers must have several times as much land available to them as they use in any single year, and they must use it in rotation. As a result, the population density of the hills can rarely match that of the plains, although the productivity of an acre of dry land during its years under cultivation may not be much lower than that of an acre of wet land. A few hill people, such as the Angami Nagas who live along the eastern borders of Assam, have built elaborate terraces on the hillsides and have been able to cultivate wet rice even in mountainous terrain; others have taken advantage of little valleys with their pockets of flat land. But most hill people rely upon dry rice. Hill farmers always grow many crops other than rice, but rice is usually as important a staple for them as it is for the farmers of the plains.

Superficially, at least to Westerners who are accustomed to dry grain agriculture, dry rice cultivation would seem to be the simpler technique, and it has often been assumed that it was the earlier form from which wet rice agriculture later developed. Like so much else about the origins of agriculture in Southeast Asia, however, there is little solid evidence for this belief. Even the location of the first domestication of rice can only be guessed at. It must have been somewhere within the area of its extensive use today—India, Southeast Asia, or China. Southeast Asia has as good a claim as any, but—except for being more centrally located—its claim is no better.

Animal domestication is as widespread as agriculture in Southeast Asia, and a few species may even have been domesticated there for the first time. The animal with the most solid claim to a Southeast Asian origin is the domestic fowl. Even the chickens of Europe and America seem to be derived from the jungle fowl that still lives in the Southeast Asian forests. The wild birds are brightly colored and smaller than their highly bred domestic cousins, but they have the same general form. In Southeast Asia fowl have been bred not only for their eggs and flesh, but also for fighting, a sport that still engrosses the attention of many. Domestic pigs have also been kept for thousands of years and were probably originally derived from the local wild pigs. Elephants are native to Southeast Asia and have long been used for labor, as a support in battle, and especially in displays of royal pomp. The people have also generally kept dogs, but this is an almost universal practice.

The traditional plants provide a diet high in starch, and domestic animals have rarely been plentiful enough to satisfy completely the other dietary needs. Southeast Asians have not exploited legumes, such as China's soybean or India's pulse, which would permit a diet low in animal protein. (This may be one reason for the lower population density of Southeast Asia.) Southeast Asians have relied more upon fish, and have developed ingenious methods of catching them. Hooks and lines, nets of many varieties, and bamboo valve traps are used almost everywhere in this area. Many people use still another technique: they dam off a section of a stream and beat a kind of bark in the water which produces a poison that stupefies the fish. Fish are often eaten fresh, but they are also regularly dried. The unaccustomed foreigner often finds the dried-fish stalls a particularly evil-smelling corner of the market, and is unlikely to be attracted by a dried-fish curry, but to Southeast Asians dried fish is an essential ingredient of the cuisine.

All these plants and animals are as old as the oldest historical records, not only in Southeast Asia but in other parts of the world as well. The theory of their Southeast Asian origin is not based on historical or archeological evidence, but upon the presence of the wild forms of these same plants and animals, and upon the more dubious observation that Southeast Asia seems to be a reasonably centralized place from which these crops and animals could have spread out to other parts of the world.*

The Origin and Development of Agriculture

The first domestication of these plants and animals is often spoken of as the Southeast Asian "Neolithic," and it has been regularly compared to the agricultural complex that grew up in the early Middle East. Of course it would be desirable to have some archaeological confirmation of early Southeast Asian agricultural development, but unfortunately there is almost none. Not only have few people bothered to dig for prehistoric remains, but what little archaeological research has been done gives hardly any solid evidence for the beginnings of agriculture. Certain archaeological remains have been *called* "Neolithic" (which today is usually understood to mean "agricultural") but the evidence for domestic crops or animals is slight.

What digging has been carried on has revealed remains that seem steadily to acquire more and more of the traits that are usually thought of as accompanying agriculture: stone tools shaped by grinding instead of by chipping, and pottery. The world has had farmers who did not have pottery or ground stone tools, and there have been hunters who used both, but they are the exceptions. As these traits become solidly established, it is increasingly difficult to imagine that their manufacturers did not also plant crops. Unfortunately this is as far as one can go, for no positive identification of domestic plants or even of domestic animals has yet been made in the archaeological remains.

Some of the most recent sites around Bac Son provide good examples of these tools. The stone celts (axe and adze heads) from the

* Many of the same plants were used by natives of the Pacific islands as far east as Hawaii. They could only have been carried there by early Polynesian settlers, who came from the west. Some of the plants are now grown as far away as West Africa, brought there, by prehistoric travelers, presumably along the shores of the Indian Ocean and into East Africa. People speaking languages related to those of Indonesia traveled as far west as Madagascar, and no doubt they were capable of reaching the coast of Africa as well. They, or others like them, may have helped to carry some of the plants out of Southeast Asia and into Africa.

latest periods are more symmetrical than the earlier ones and, for the first time, some are ground smooth over their entire surface. This gives them a strikingly different appearance from the earlier tools. These celts are often square, rectangular, or trapezoidal in cross section, and their smooth surfaces join at sharply defined edges. The working edge is often neatly beveled. Many of them have a tang of some sort at the base which was presumably designed to allow the tool to be hafted to a handle. The tools vary considerably, but they are all strikingly different from the far coarser and more irregular celts found around Hoa Binh.

A site called Nga-Trang in central Vietnam has yielded masterful examples of this sort. Some of the celts are as much as a foot long, but hardly two inches wide or thick. Rectangular in cross section, they are beveled at the working end and gently taper toward the other end where there is the hint of a tang. They must rank among the most skillfully made ground stone tools that man ever produced. Celts of this general type, though rarely so flawlessly constructed, have been found over much of Southeast Asia and in eastern India, southern China, and some of the adjacent Pacific islands as well—most of them in places where dating is impossible. An attempt has been made to categorize these celts according to form of their cross sections or to the presence or absence of a tang, and some scholars have tried to guess their relative age. It has often been claimed that they were invented somewhere else—perhaps in China—and carried southward by successive waves of immigrants, though the evidence for this claim is minimal. The most that can be said with assurance is that at one time these quadrangular celts were used over most of Southeast Asia, and they must have been used more recently than the cruder chipped tools of the hoabinhian type. It is likely that they were used right up until the introduction of metal, possibly as late as the time of Christ.

Other stone objects seem to be about as old as the celts. Stone rings a few inches in diameter have been found in both Vietnam and Malaya. Any imaginative archaeologist might guess that those were bracelets but in this case his guesses would be confirmed, for human skeletons have been found with stone rings still encircling the bones of the arms. The rings were made by drilling the stone with square-cut pieces of bamboo (with sand used as an abrasive to assist the wearing action). In this way the craftsman could cut out a plug of stone and, with a smaller piece of bamboo, drill a smaller plug from its center. The many center plugs and unfinished specimens that have been found clearly demonstrate the technique of manufacture.

Stone objects with a square butt marked with engraved crosshatching have been found in Malaya. The form of these objects is remarkably similar to that of bark cloth beaters which are still used in a few places, though most of the modern ones are made of wood. Perhaps these ancient people already used bark cloth.

Contemporaneously with the manufacture of these stone objects, pottery becomes reasonably abundant for the first time. Pottery from earlier periods has been found at Bac Son and even at Hoa Binh, but it is abundant only from the latest period at Bac Son, when it is characteristically decorated with incised, cord-marked, or mat-marked designs. Pottery and ground stone tools occur together in Malaya, too, and here also the pottery is sometimes cord-marked, and occasionally incised, though the surface ornamentation is rarely elaborate. The potters of that period exercised their imagination in the elaborate and flamboyant shapes they produced. Some of the pieces have stands; others have round bottoms, straight sides, or sinuous indentations of various sorts. Most are quite wide-mouthed —dishes or large bowls. Little objects shaped like distorted doughnuts and concave on top and bottom have been called *pot stands.* They could hardly have been used as containers for they have holes through their centers, but they might have been set on the floor to support round-bottomed pots that could not stand up by themselves.

One famous archaeological site deserves special mention: Samrong Sen in Cambodia. The findings at Samrong Sen have been variously called "Neolithic" or even "Bronze Age," although the evidence of metal is doubtful and there is no incontestable evidence of agriculture. The site has yielded objects typologically similar to the later bacsonian period, including quadrangular ground stone celts, stone bracelets, and elaborate pottery. Samrong Sen, however, has yielded a few things which are rare or absent in the other sites. These include bone and shell objects and a number of trinkets that may have been used as jewelry. There are rings and pendants of mollusk shell, some looking like big buttons except that they have only one hole (for wearing on a string, perhaps). There are circular decorated objects, some made of pottery, some of large fish vertebrae. These are thought to have been inserted into distended earlobes, for similar ornaments are still worn by a few people. They usually have a rather distinctive cruciform design and are about an inch and a half in diameter. Little shell objects an inch or so in length with a hole at each end may have been used as beads or pendants, and there are a few bone points, some of which may possibly have been harpoon heads.

Visitors to Samrong Sen have also found a few small bronze objects: little bells, a fish hook, a simple ring, and something looking like a chisel. Unfortunately, these all seem to have been purchased from nearby villagers and did not come directly from the site. The villagers may well have recognized a good thing and sold the bronze pieces by claiming that they came from the site. No competent archaeologist has ever found bronze *in situ* at Samrong Sen, probably because the people did not use it.

Pottery and ground stone celts have been widely found in Southeast Asia, and though few sites have been excavated with enough care to give any idea of how long ago these objects were made (guesses run to three or four thousand years), a widespread population seems to have had an expert knowledge of both pottery manufacture and stone-grinding techniques. In other parts of the world these traits are usually found among agricultural peoples. But although the pottery and the beautifully worked stone celts would seem to indicate that the people who made them must also have been planting fields, this cannot be confirmed until more systematic excavations have been made.

It is not impossible that these ground stone tools and pottery were made by farmers who also learned to domesticate the plants and animals considered to be part of the Southeast Asian "Neolithic," but only the bark cloth beaters (if that is really what they were) show any real similarity to the traits presumed to have belonged to the "Neolithic" complex. Connecting the remains with the hypothetical Neolithic brings order into the data, but when better archaeological evidence at last appears, any premature ordering that we insist upon today is likely to appear grossly over-simplified.

Somewhat surprisingly, the time of the arrival of metal in South-east Asia is almost as obscure as the origin of agriculture. All the people of the mainland have used metal throughout their known history, but nobody believes that the manufacture of metal was developed locally. In fact metal is the first of many traits which can be attributed with some confidence to the influence of another area.

Bronze, and later iron, were first used in the Middle East and the knowledge of their manufacture spread out from there in all directions. Their spread southeast into India and northeast into China can be clearly documented and the first bronze objects of Southeast Asia are enough like those of China to make most people conclude that the knowledge of bronze came from the north, first, perhaps, with the importing of finished bronze objects and later through the spread of the technical knowledge necessary for manufacture. The piece with the clearest Chinese antecedents is a characteristic type of socketed bronze celt. Its outline is much like that of the body of a violin, but one end tapers to a sharpened edge and the other has a socket for a handle. Similar celts have been found in China and even in Siberia, but they are unknown in India or the Middle East.

Beautiful big pieces known as kettledrums have also been found. They have a tympanum as large as two feet in diameter and are set on metal bases. These drums are elaborately ornamented with geometric designs or with pictures, some realistic, others stylized representations of animals, people, houses, and boats. The drums are remarkably similar to the brass drums and gongs which are still prized as valuable heirlooms and as symbols of wealth and status by many tribal people. The modern owners rarely know just where or by whom their drums and gongs were manufactured. The people who use them today prize them as antiques, but certainly not all the pieces date from the early Bronze Age. Nevertheless, an unbroken continuity ties them to the Bronze Age drums.

The early metal objects are only rarely found in a condition that permits accurate dating. Because of their stylistic similarities to the more accurately datable objects from the Bronze Age in China, it is generally supposed that bronze was first used in Southeast Asia in the centuries just before the birth of Christ. In the Middle East the manufacture of iron began almost two thousand years later than that of bronze, but it spread more rapidly and it may have followed the earlier technique into Southeast Asia within only a few centuries. Like the knowledge of bronze manufacture, the knowledge of iron manufacture could have come south from China, but it may also have come from India. Certainly contact between Southeast Asia and India goes back at least to the early centuries after Christ. From that time also come the first historical records from Southeast Asia, so the Iron Age merges with the beginnings of the historical era.

Metals were not the only traits to diffuse into Southeast Asia. Cows and water buffalo were probably first imported from India, but Southeast Asians are more likely than Indians to eat the flesh of these animals, and far less likely to drink their milk. Horses probably came from China, and they are used widely in the northern hills, though they are not common elsewhere. Foreign plants were also imported to supplement the indigenous ones. Many crops of the dry Middle East cannot be grown in the humid Southeast Asian climate, and the crops of Europe are often unsuited to the heat, though considerable quantities of wheat are grown in the hills of Burma and especially in Yunnan. The most important new crops were to come from the Americas. Parts of tropical America are as wet as Southeast Asia and its plants have been readily adopted. The most important of these is Indian corn or maize. It is not known exactly how maize found its way into Southeast Asia, but it must have done so remarkably soon after ships first joined the Old and the New Worlds, for today maize of many different varieties is grown in the most inaccessible mountain areas of Southeast Asia, and the people have no memory that it is a less ancient crop than rice or taro. Manioc, another New World crop, is a tuber from which tapioca is made; it can also be roasted or boiled. Potatoes are grown in some hill areas, though they do not thrive in the lowlands. Tobacco, a plant which can grow under extraordinarily diverse conditions, was long ago introduced to the most remote corners of Southeast Asia. Chili peppers have been taken into the native diet with such enthusiasm that it is now difficult to imagine what the cuisine could have been like before the discovery of America led to their importation and local adaptation.

Metal and some of these new crops are as useful in the hills as in the plains. A hill man can find as much work for an iron axe as a plains man can, and he may be able to grow some crops even more successfully. Any trait that could be used in the hills was adopted so quickly that there was no appreciable time lag between their use in the plains and their spread into the hills. The only traits that the hills did not adopt were those which they could not successfully use, such as wet rice agriculture.

Once iron had arrived, the Southeast Asian hill people had all the prerequisites necessary for the kind of life still led there. By about two thousand years ago, hill people could clear fields as efficiently as they do now. Bamboo could be worked, baskets made, and houses built. Many of the same plants could be grown, though new plants have since been added. This technology could have supported much the same sort of social behavior that it still supports, so the kind of life that is now typical of the hills is likely to have been pretty well established by the time of Christ. Of course the details must have changed—people have migrated, and even those who stayed in one place must have thought up new ways of organizing their lives—but the essential features of life have probably been reasonably constant.

An examination of a few specific tribes will provide a fuller view of the possibilities for life in the hills. No more than the Andamanese or Malayan Negritos are these tribes the direct and unchanged descendants of the aboriginal inhabitants, but they can provide examples of the kind of life which has long been possible in the hills.

Chapter Four

The Hill People

The Garos

On the westernmost fringe of Southeast Asia, in the hills south of the Brahmaputra River in Assam, lives a tribe whose members call themselves simply *A'chik,* or *hill men,* but who are known to everyone else as *Garos.* In many respects they and the other people who live in the hills surrounding the valley of Assam are more like Southeast Asians than like the other people of India. The Garo language belongs to the Tibeto-Burman family, and the Garos themselves, being predominantly Mongoloid, look more like Southeast Asians than like most of their Indian compatriots. They are not Hindu and they lack all the intricate customs associated with the Indian caste system. The Garos and the other hill people of Assam are an exotic and peculiar minority in India, but they would hardly be out of place among the hill people of Burma or Vietnam.

About a quarter of a million Garos live in a compact district in southwestern Assam, and within their district they form the predominant population. The district is criss-crossed by valleys and low ridges, but the mountains do not reach so high as in other parts in Assam or as in some other regions of Southeast Asia. Most of the district is less than three thousand feet above sea level. Outsiders are often surprised to learn that this elevation is the most favorable for mosquitoes of the genus *Anopheles,* and hence for malaria, but the local people have never had any doubt. Until about a century ago, both plains Indians and Britons were justifiably terrified of the chills and fevers so prevalent in the hills. Their fear, together with the difficulty of moving through the hills with their few roads and many hostile inhabitants, effectively protected the Garos' independence. About a century ago, quinine, better weapons, and more effective road-building techniques combined to allow the British government to occupy the Garo country and to bring an end to their independence, but even today the Garos retain their distinctive way of life.

By Indian standards, the hills have a wealth of resources. Because population density is much lower in Garo country than in most of India, there are more wild products and uncultivated sources of food available. The forests are filled with wild animals: jungle fowl, deer, pigs, gibbons, monkeys (both langur and macaque), tigers, leopards, snakes, and elephants. The elephants (which the Garos greatly fear) are now strictly protected by the Indian government, for they are an important and increasingly rare natural resource, but to the Garos, forbidden to kill them and defenseless against their encroachment, they are often a nuisance and occasionally a danger. They invade fields, trample crops and even knock over small buildings, either to reach stores of grain or, it seems, in sheer mischief. Garos fish in the streams and hunt deer and jungle fowl in the forests. They collect a few wild plants to supplement their diet. The bulk of their food, however, comes from their fields.

Early each year the Garos clear a new patch of land and let it dry until the end of March, when they burn the cuttings which they have left scattered about. (At this time of the year the weather is so parched that the fields burn easily and rapidly.) The planting is begun early in the morning after the fire, for the Garos feel that it must be done while the blackened ash can still blow over the seeds and promote their growth. Many of the crops are planted by broadcasting. Instead of planting each crop in its own separate plot the farmer deliberately mixes the seeds of all species before he scatters them about the fields. Later, other crops which cannot be planted by broadcasting are also distributed over the entire field. As a result millet, maize, taro, yams, chili peppers, cotton, ginger, and a score of other foods come up thoroughly intermixed. A farmer from the West would find this a disorderly way to plant, but it is an efficient way to make maximum use of the land. This is because the climate allows a very long growing season, and different types of crops, though all planted in March and April, ripen from June until the following December or January, so that crops are removed from the fields nearly continuously over a six-month period. The early crops have enough space to grow because the late crops are still small. By the time the late crops need the space, the earlier ones are harvested and gone. By planting a wide variety of crops, moreover, the Garos insure themselves against the failure of any particular species.

After the planting is finished, the hardest work is to keep down the weeds. Planting is timed to take advantage of the rains, but the rains also encourage dozens of varieties of weeds. These must be painstakingly extracted from the fields, or they will rapidly choke out the crops. When the cotton (the last crop to ripen) has been harvested, the fields are cleaned once again.

The next year the fields are used exclusively for rice, the only proper staple and an essential part of every meal. The rice is planted, a few grains at a time, in little holes made with a pointed dibble. The rice field must also be continuously cultivated to keep down the weeds. The rice is usually harvested in September, and then, after two seasons of use, the fertility of the fields is so reduced that they are abandoned to weeds and jungle. No more crops are grown on them for eight or ten years, when the cycle is repeated. Because the Garos clear new fields each year and keep each field in use for two years, they always cultivate two separate fields during any single growing season—one planted with a great variety of crops, the other devoted exclusively to rice.

Garos also keep a few animals. Cattle are the most highly valued of these, though they are never milked and traditionally are not used for plowing or for drawing carts. A cow's value derives from the possibility of its becoming the basis of a feast. In the absence of refrigeration, a cow must be eaten within two or three days of its slaughter and this is more than a single family can manage, even with their small cows, but Garos find many reasons to assemble a crowd large enough to consume a whole animal. A cow is killed with ceremony: it is ritually sacrificed and some of its blood is offered to the spirits, but the sacrifice is always followed by a feast. Garos also keep pigs and chickens. They eat the eggs, but they also use both pigs and chickens for sacrifices not important enough to warrant the loss of a cow.

Few agricultural peoples, and probably none in Southeast Asia, have tried to organize their farming in any way except by dividing the work among the families. Garos apportion the agricultural land among the households, and the members of each household have primary responsibility for their own plot. They plant, cultivate, and harvest their crops and they may use them as they see fit. Because the Garos, like the other hill people in Southeast Asia, regularly abandon exhausted old fields, new land must be frequently distributed. Everyone who lives in a Garo village has the right to claim a new plot of the village land each year, and to that extent it can be said that Garos have certain communal rights to the land, but once the land is distributed, each household works on its special plot and organizes its work as it pleases. Of course, the growing season and the characteristics of their crops impose a regular pattern upon the work. The sharp seasonal concentration of rain forces everyone to plant and to harvest at the same time of year. Yet the Garos synchronize their work even more than the seasons demand, for their agricultural cycle is punctuated by a series of villagewide ceremonies. Garos often trade labor with one another, so they do spend many days working on someone else's land. Two friends may each work for a day on the other's plot, simply because the work is more pleasant that way and seems to go more quickly. Sometimes all the people from two or three households help each other when the work is heaviest, but no amount of labor exchange can override the unique rights and responsibility of each family toward its own particular plot.

Although the responsibility taken by each family toward its plot is characteristic of all Southeast Asian farmers, the way in which the families themselves are organized is extremely variable. Nothing about the Garo family organization can be regarded as typical, and indeed, in many ways it is unique. Many Garo households include only a married couple and their children, but others are larger. When a Garo couple grows old enough to find the burden of the household work difficult, they must persuade another, younger couple to live with them. They manage this by appointing one of their daughters as their "heiress." The couple's other children move away when they marry, but this girl's husband must come to live in her parents' house. As a result households often include two married couples but rarely more. The heiress and her husband (who can be called the "heir") have several unique privileges and responsibilities. They inherit all the property of the girl's parents, including the house, standing crops and stored grain, tools, clothing, and such heirlooms as jewelry or brass gongs. Sons and other daughters receive nothing. Of course some men share the inheritance of their wives, but the other daughters and their husbands must start from scratch to build up a new household of their own. Garos do not look upon this as inequitable, because however old, senile, and useless for work the girl's parents become, the heiress and her husband must work to support them. Such a burden may more than offset the advantages of the inheritance.

The property which is left to the heir and heiress includes the large and comfortable bamboo house the Garos build. These houses may be as much as fifty or even seventy-five feet long, but are rarely more than fifteen feet wide. The house is often divided into several rooms. At the front there may be a room with a packed-earth floor where the cattle are tethered and household goods stored. The other rooms have split-bamboo floors built well off the ground. The main room has a central fireplace where food is cooked and around which the family and their friends can sit on cool winter evenings. A separate room may be partitioned off at the back for the oldest couple, but small families often manage with a single room.

The entrance to the house is at one end and there, under wide eaves, the women do much of the household work. One of their heaviest jobs is pounding rice. The rice grain comes off the stalk encased in a tough husk. This must be broken and the rice grain removed. Everywhere in Southeast Asia, people have some technique for pounding the grain to break the husk. The Garos make a mortar from the cross section of a large tree trunk, into which they carve a hole a few inches in diameter to hold the rice. A large pole is the pestle, and the woman pounds it repeatedly into this pile of rice. This breaks the husk, and the rice can then be tossed into the air from a winnowing basket. The husk, being lighter than the grain, blows away, while the grain falls back into the basket. Pounding rice is a time-consuming and tiring job, but it is an inescapable duty of every Garo housewife.

Among traditional Garos the girl or her parents choose her future husband. When they have picked out a likely boy, the girl's father calls upon several of the youths of their village to capture him and bring him to his bride. The boys sneak into the bridegroom's village or lie in wait in the jungle to surprise him as he innocently walks down a path. When they see their chance, they seize him. The groom need know nothing of his impending capture until the minute the boys set upon him, though of course every Garo boy of marriageable age recognizes the peril under which he lives, and any boy worth his salt puts up a battle, and tries to run away. But he is always outnumbered and sooner or later must admit defeat and allow himself to be led to the house of the girl. There, without asking his permission, a wedding ceremony is held. A cock and a hen are killed and are allowed to flop about on the floor of the house as their life departs. If the birds finally come to rest with their heads pointing toward each other, this is taken as a good sign for the marriage, but if their heads should point in opposite directions, this is taken as a bad sign. Whatever the omen, this constitutes the wedding ceremony, and if the boy decides to stay and settle down as a husband, a new marriage begins.

However, boys are expected to want to leave, even after the ceremony is finished. They seldom stay the first time they are "taken," but they cannot simply stand and walk away, for their captors watch them far too closely. The ceremony is usually held in the evening, and when it is time to sleep the captors insist that the boy sleep next to the back wall of the house and share the bride's blankets. The captors then array themselves about the couple so as to frustrate any escape attempt the boy might make. The public nature of the wedding night makes consummation of the marriage impossible; in any event, the groom is often interested primarily in escape. It is impossible for the captors to stay awake all night every night and, sooner or later, their guard must fall and the boy finds his chance to flee. If he runs home, he is temporarily free, but unless he announces clearly and publicly that he will have nothing more to do with this girl, he may be recaptured later. By that time, he will have had a chance to consider the proposal carefully and he may then decide to settle down and live with her. Occasionally a couple may first reach a private agreement, but the bridegroom is "kidnapped" anyway. Usually, however, the boy must wait to be chosen by the girl.

Even a girl who has not been chosen as heiress usually lives with her husband in her own village, often near her parents' house. The boy may be captured from a village several miles distant, but it is he who must move. This means that, in any given village, the women are usually closely related while their husbands are assembled from all the villages within a radius of six or eight miles. The new household of a nonheiress and her husband is spoken of as "coming out" of the household of her mother, while the heiress takes over the older household intact. The two households are economically distinct. They build separate houses, work separate fields, and cook their food separately, but of course the girl, her sisters, and their mother—living close together—continue to help each other. Similarly, the husbands of the two sisters, though usually related only through their wives, often help each other by exchanging labor in the fields or by helping to build one another's houses. As the sisters grow old, their own children mature and each sister will eventually appoint a daughter as heiress and will be joined by a son-in-law. If one sister should have no daughter, but another sister has two, one girl may move to her aunt's house to act as her heiress, for it is unthinkable that anyone should grow old without having his own heir and heiress to care for him.

Because each generation usually has more girls than the last, the set of related households gradually expands. For many generations Garos continue to calculate their important relatives among these households of related women. Husbands come in from other households and villages, and the maternal uncles, the brothers, and the sons of the women leave to marry elsewhere. Each set of women, therefore has ties with two sets of men, their inmarrying husbands and their outmarrying brothers. Similarly, each man has ties both with the set of households into which he was born and with that of his wife and daughters, and they have responsibilities in both directions. Although many brothers may move away to another village, they all retain a responsibility toward their sisters and their families. If a woman feels that her husband is neglecting her, she can call upon her brother to defend her, but if a husband shows his wife to be guilty of adultery, for instance, her brother is expected to help punish her.

The day-to-day discipline of small children is left to their mother and father, but parents will sometimes threaten the children with their mother's brother, and in serious matters—especially after the children reach adolescence—the maternal uncle is actually asked to provide discipline. If a sixteen-year-old boy should steal something, it is never the father but the mother's brother or another of the mother's male kinsmen who imposes the punishment. In other words, although the brothers and uncles of a group of related women do not take day-to-day responsibility for running the households of their sisters and nieces, their help is solicited whenever an important decision must be made. The set of kinsmen who are related to each other through women, and who are descended from a common ancestress, are known as a "matrilineal lineage." A tribe in which kinship is traced through the female line, can be called matrilineal, but it is clear that the Garos have no matriarchy, for the women do not rule.

Though women do not govern or direct the men, this family system does give women certain advantages. Because they usually remain in the same village throughout their lives, they are always surrounded by a group of close kinsmen who provide a security and continuity that would be lacking if the women had to go and live in their husbands' households or villages. Garo women are certainly "free" in the sense that they have an important voice in the running of their own households and in their complete lack of seclusion. Their behavior differs from that of the women in many parts of India who are relatively secluded within their houses, and who can never speak freely with unrelated men. Garo women go by themselves to work in their fields; they go to the market, where they help to buy and sell; they participate in all family decisions. Nevertheless, they are dependent upon men—not only their husbands but their brothers and maternal uncles as well,

The manner in which the women of a Garo village are related implies that one household in each village will be considered to have seniority. Every other household has "come out" from that household. whether recently or several generations earlier. The man who marries into this senior household rates the title of *nokma,* and he has special responsibilities toward the village. His heir, who will be the next *nokma,* is chosen just as are all other heirs—by being captured and then married to a chosen daughter. As this youth grows older, and especially after his father-in-law dies, he becomes responsible for several ceremonies which mark points in the agricultural calendar and insure the well-being of the village and the success of the crops. The *nokma* can never belong to the same lineage as most of the women and children of his village, for it is strictly forbidden to marry a woman of one's own lineage. Thus his important responsibilities are always directed toward a lineage other than his own.

If the *nokma* is an able and aggressive man, he is often an influential member of the village. Garos claim that, in the past, *nokmas* led them on headhunting expeditions; more recently, the government has given them such duties as looking after traveling officials and organizing work parties to clear the paths between villages. Garos also claim that, before their district was taken over by the British, the *nokma* was the man who settled their disputes. Whether or not this was ever true, it is not true now: today legal cases are settled by arbitration between the kinsmen of the disputants with an appointed government representative sitting as a neutral magistrate. This representative helps the parties to reach a decision, and he puts the government stamp of approval upon it.

One of the commonest disputes among the Garos concerns adultery, for not all Garos are strictly faithful to their spouses. If a woman should be unfaithful to her husband, his recourse is not to violence; rather, he sues the lover. The husband, his wife, the lover, and the kinsmen of all three meet together to try to agree on the facts of the case and to decide what must be done. Garo women do not seem skillful at hiding the facts in such situations, and if it is clear that the husband's accusations are just, traditional punishments should be imposed. The kinsmen of the lover are expected to pay a monetary compensation to the kinsmen of the husband. This punishes the lover's family for having allowed their kinsman to behave so badly, and demonstrates—by their willingness to pay over the money—their own good will and their remorse over their kinsman's transgression. They are also expected to punish the kinsman who has brought them so much trouble, and they do this by leading him outdoors and vigorously thrashing him. Because kinsmen are always responsible for each other's acts, everyone knows that his own behavior is being watched and that if he steps too far out of line, his kinsmen will be waiting to punish him. This mutual responsibility certainly helps to keep Garos well-behaved, for it is hard to be wicked with all one's relatives watching.

Whatever the crime, a monetary compensation is supposed to settle it. A convicted thief must not only return what he has stolen, but his family must pay a compensation to the family of the victim. One shown to have falsely accused another owes him compensation. The family of a murderer turns over a large sum of money for distribution among the kinsmen of his victim, although today the government also locks up the murderer. In the past, a murder was more likely to be punished by another murder, and a feud could lead to intervillage warfare and headhunting raids. Today headhunting is only a memory, and monetary compensation is supposed to end any dispute. To accept the money is to agree to the settlement and to renounce any further claim. Adultery, for instance, does not necessarily lead to divorce, and many Garo couples live in apparent harmony for many years after one of them has been convicted of adultery and paid the appropriate compensation.

Divorce, nevertheless, is not unknown. Marriage is expected to be permanent, but Garos do not expect a couple to stay together if they can no longer bear each other's company. Divorce is probably no more common among Garos than among Americans, but it is far less complicated to bring about. Whenever the husband or wife can bear it no longer, he or she can end the marriage. There need be no grounds and no formal accusation against the spouse. A man usually leaves the house; a woman evicts her husband. But whoever initiates the divorce owes a compensation to the abandoned spouse and, like any other compensation, the amount is negotiated at a meeting of the kinsmen of the litigants. One side collects the compensation and distributes it among the other.

Garos are a reasonably worldly people. Within the limits of their technology, they are skillful farmers and attack their daily problems with considerable rationality, but for problems too great to cope with, they may seek supernatural solutions. For instance, crops usually grow as expected, but they do occasionally fail. To help forestall such a possibility, Garos carry out a regular series of ceremonies. At some of these, each household sacrifices an animal and offers its blood and some rice beer to the gods in the hope that they will look kindly upon the crops. At other ceremonies only the *nokma* offers the sacrifice, but the objective is the same. Garo gods require no solemnity and the ceremonies are made the occasion of exciting festivals which may last for several days, during which large amounts of rice beer help keep everyone in a joyful mood.

Another problem which Garos have been unable to deal with rationally is disease. The Garo hills are an unhealthy place. Besides malaria, there is the usual collection of tropical dysenteries. Cholera and other diseases occasionally become epidemic. Infant mortality is particularly high; it is a fortunate woman who manages to raise half her children to adulthood. Garos have, from the point of view of modern medicine, been relatively helpless in the face of sickness and death. They do not take sickness idly, but try to drive it away by animal sacrifices. Disease is attributed to the "bite" of spirits or *mite,* as the Garos call them. Garos cannot describe the *mite* clearly but they are certain that they do men no good. The bite of each *mite* causes its own characteristic symptoms, and by observing the symptoms one can determine which *mite* to blame and what kind of sacrifice to perform. Each *mite* requires its own special ritual. A new altar is always built, the form of which depends on the spirit at fault, and anything from an egg to a cow may be offered the spirit in the hope of driving him away. Usually a half-dozen kinsmen and neighbors help with the sacrifices, after which the animal is always cooked and eaten. Fortunately, a sacrifice is usually effective, and within a few days the sick person's health improves. Sometimes it takes longer and a series of sacrifices may be necessary. Occasionally no sacrifice is effective—some spirits are too strong for the people to drive away—and the victim then dies. Garos know that their defense against these evil spirits is limited.

Garos believe that after a man dies his soul goes off to another world, though eventually it may be born again into this world. To speed him to the other world, Garos cremate the body on a pyre of wooden poles—and if his friends and kinsmen are rich enough, they sacrifice a few cows for him to take along.

A hundred years ago the Garos were independent of foreign rule, but they were never completely isolated from the people around them. Their language has absorbed hundreds of words from the languages of the Indian plains. Like other Southeast Asian hill tribes, they long ago acquired iron tools to clear their forests and to make their delicate bamboo baskets and sturdy houses. New crops that could be adapted to their terrain were readily taken over—among them, maize, manioc, and tobacco. From the time of the earliest historical records, and perhaps for many hundreds of years before that, Garos have traveled to markets in the plains to sell their crops and to purchase goods that the plains people could offer. The caste system, the Hindu religion, and—until a century ago—organized government stopped at the foot of the hills, but for the last hundred years the Garos have been incorporated into India. Since then, roads have been built and new market places established, so that few villages are more than a few hours' walk from a market. Here Garos sell their cash crops—cotton, ginger, chili peppers, oranges, and pineapples—all of which grow well in the hills and find a ready market in the plains. With their money, they buy mill cloth (weaving is almost a lost art), iron tools, jewelry, and even such essential foods as salt and dried fish.

A district government has been established which forbids local warfare and which must approve the settlement of each serious dispute, though it allows them to be settled according to Garo custom. The decisions of the village courts can be appealed to district courts and, in principle, even to the high court of Assam. Under the constitution of independent India, the Garos now elect a local district council which has assumed many governmental functions and has been led predominantly by elected Garos. The electorate has also sent several Garos to the state legislature at Shillong, and the Garos have participated in national elections. The Garos' interest in politics has been rising, but their main concern is still with local problems and with their relations to the other people of the state of Assam.

The establishment of peace has allowed new religious doctrines to penetrate the hills. Western missionaries have had only limited success among Hindus, Buddhists, or Muslims, but they have done better among people like the Garos who had never participated in any of these highly systematized religious traditions. Peace, and contact with a broader world have brought new problems to which Christian missionaries seemed to offer solutions. Missionaries brought education and medicine and won some converts through their example of service, but they may also have won converts among Garos who saw in Christianity a means of moral defense against the plains people. Garos have lived for hundreds of years without being absorbed by the plains people, but military conquest from the plains brought with it the threat of cultural conquest as well. To some Garos, Christianity has seemed to offer an alternative. At any rate, about one third of the Garos have become Christians, and Christianity continues to make steady advances among the rest. Converts abandon the more obvious aspects of their old religion: the sacrifices and the funeral practices. Whether they completely give up their belief in spirits may be doubted, but they are more apt to take Western medicine than are those who retain explicit faith in the spirit theory of disease. Christian Garos build churches, sing hymns, and begin to show an interest in persuading others to adopt their new religion.

The Lamets

The Lamet tribe lives several hundred miles east of the Garos in the northwest corner of Laos, not far from the borders of Thailand and Burma. Thanks to the excellent reporting of the Swedish ethnographer, K. G. Izikowitz, they can be described in fuller detail than most Southeast Asian tribes. The Lamets are fewer in number than the Garos and their villages are closer to those of their neighbors. In fact, although the Laotian province in which they live is only about two hundred and fifty miles in diameter, no less than twenty-five different languages are spoken there. Laotian itself is spoken by lowlanders and traders, but languages of the Tibeto-Burman, Thai, and Mon-Khmer families are spoken by other people. The Lamet language itself is one of the Mon-Khmer group. This extraordinary ethnic scrambling is typical of the country north of the plains of Thailand, but it hardly has a parallel anywhere else in the world. The Lamets themselves number something under four thousand. They live in mountainous country, and their villages are usually built in areas which lie at between 1500 and 3000 feet above sea level. Much the same variety of wild animals fill their jungles as fill those of the Garos: everything from leeches to elephants.

About seventy inches of rain fall on the Lamet country each year, only about half as much as the Garo hills receive, but it comes at the same time of year and imposes the same seasonal pattern upon agriculture. In March the Lamets burn their cleared patches of jungle, repair their tools, and tighten their belts, for at this time of year few wild plants or animals can be found, and the harvest of the previous year may be almost entirely gone. By the end of April they start planting, and after the monsoon begins in June, bamboo shoots and then many other wild plants help to eke out their diet until the harvest. By July and August, maize, manioc, cucumbers, taro, and sweet potatoes are ready, and by the end of September the earliest rice is harvested. Lamet agriculture is technologically simple, for it depends entirely upon slash-and-burn methods and involves neither plows nor irrigation. The Lamets cultivate a patch of land for a single year and plant all their crops together. Each year they put up a temporary building in their fields where they live during much of the growing season, and in this way avoid having to commute back and forth to the village each day.

The Lamets have a number of ceremonies which are associated with the agricultural cycle, and they perform sacrifices in honor of the village spirits. The ceremonies center upon rice which, alone among the crops, is believed to have a soul. The rice soul must be enticed to stay with the crop, so at harvest-time, the Lamets erect altars at crossroads in order to persuade the rice soul to take the path that leads to the fields, and after each section of the fields has been harvested, they "lead" the soul on to the next section. Because the soul is thought to be unable to find its way across open spaces, it must be enticed across paths or openings. Later, more rites must be conducted to make certain that the soul stays in the barns with the rice, otherwise the supply will soon be exhausted, and famine will follow.

The fields are not the only source of food. Collecting wild plants from the jungle is more important for the Lamets than for the Garos, and jungle crops add considerable variety to their diet. The Lamets keep a few permanent gardens near their villages, and they grow a few tea plants in the jungle, so as to obtain tea leaves to ferment and chew. They have fruit trees, including areca palms, the nuts of which are wrapped in the leaves of the betel vine and smeared with lime to make a small edible packet. Chewing this mixture stimulates the flow of bright red saliva, which eventually leaves the teeth with a dark stain considered unattractive by most Europeans. But the Lamets, like most Southeast Asians, find the betel mixture satisfying (somewhat as tobacco can be) and it is widely offered to guests as a gesture of hospitality.

The Lamets also keep buffalo, cattle, pigs, chickens, dogs, and bees, and eat the flesh of all (except the bees). The animals run loose about the village, and, like many other Southeast Asians, the Lamets build fences around the fields to keep the animals out, rather than build fences around the animals to keep them in. The Lamets also fish with traps and with nets, and they hunt with crossbows. Crossbows must have originally been imported from China, but they have now been taken over by many people of northern Southeast Asia. The bow is held horizontal and cocked; then the arrow is released by a trigger. Crossbows are highly effective weapons for they can have a stronger spring and can be aimed more carefully than a simple bow.

Both men and women work in the fields. Women do the domestic jobs: they collect wild plants, firewood, and water, and they cook the family's food. Men make the tools, the weapons, and the baskets, and they do the heaviest work of clearing the fields. Men also take care of the buffalo, but women care for the pigs and chickens.

Each family has its own house, a rectangular bamboo structure with the floor built high off the ground so that animals and equipment may be stored beneath. At the front of the house there are steps leading up to a veranda, from which a door opens into the main room of the house. Within the room, one side is lined with sleeping platforms; on the other are the cooking hearth and an altar erected in honor of the family's ancestors. Sacrifices are made from time to time at the altar, and flowers are offered here to the soul of rice. In the rear corner of the room is a special sleeping platform for marriageable girls.

Most families also own smaller buildings which serve as both storehouses and worksheds. Unlike the houses, they are usually built at ground level. Tools are both manufactured and stored in these outbuildings, and people may even live in them temporarily while building a real house. Not all families have a workshed, and those that do not can use a community building to store their tools and to sit and work in the company of their neighbors. Families also own their own granaries, and if a granary is close enough to the village, it may be used for working and for storing tools as well as grain.

A household consists of a man, his wife or wives and their children, and it sometimes includes the wives and children of one or more of his sons, as well. A daughter and her husband sometimes live temporarily with her parents, while the husband does "bride service" (work to repay the debt he owes her family for giving him a wife). Large families with several married children are admired but difficult to maintain, for after several years of marriage sons often set up a separate household with their wives. Before a young man can become independent, he must first clear some land of his own, and he will need a bountiful harvest before he can persuade other villagers to help him build his new house, for the owner must always supply helpers with food.

Each family clears land in the neighborhood of the village for its own fields, and each cares for its own animals and its own trees. When an animal is slaughtered, however, the meat is usually widely distributed. A single family could not possibly eat a whole buffalo, but because large animals are usually slaughtered only on ceremonial occasions, they become the basis of feasts to which many people are invited. The products of the fields belong to the household that cleared the land and worked the crops. Each family decides how much work it should do, how much land to clear, and what proportion of its crops to eat, to sell, or to use for winning prestige.

Prestige is gained by sacrificing to the ancestors, but only a man who has worked hard and invested skillfully can hope to become rich enough to make the required sacrifices. He needs at least one hard-working wife, and the labor of a second wife is helpful. The peak productivity of the household comes after the children are mature but before they have moved away to set up their own households. An ambitious man can invest in buffalos and hope that they will multiply each year, though regular sacrifices and the occasional disbursements to obtain wives for his sons will drain away some of his herd. As he builds up his wealth, a man can buy bronze drums (the most prestigious sign of affluence) and then try to gain a reputation as an intermediary in disputes. For each dispute he settles he will receive a fee. The richest men are those who own many buffalo and bronze drums, and they are known as *Lem*. They form a highly respected group, almost a nobility, though their status is not necessarily hereditary. A man who becomes rich enough will be honored at a feast put on by the other *Lem* of the village, and be allowed to don a new silk turban. Henceforth he too will be called a *Lem*. The *Lem* can usually claim the best land. At feasts they receive the biggest portions of meat and are the first to be served rice beer, so once a man becomes a *Lem* his status brings material rewards as well as the admiration of the other villagers. But to become a *Lem* and to keep his position, a man must hold regular feasts, and if he should ever lose his wealth his rank, too, will be lost.

Marriage among the Lamets is preceded by a long and intimate courtship. A young man and his sweetheart may sit and chat on the veranda of her house until everyone else is asleep and then retire to the girls' sleeping platform. After the couple have agreed to marry, both families must meet to decide upon the formalities. Normally, the boy's family pays a bride price to the girl's parents, although a poor man may be able to avoid this by living at his bride's house for a while and working off the price on his father-in-law's fields. The bride price may consist of two to four buffalos, a few gongs, and—though rarely—a bronze drum. When the children of *Lem* marry, the bride price is higher, and a man can boost his own prestige by paying an especially high price for his wife. This usually prevents a poor man from marrying the daughter of a *Lem*, though the son of a *Lem*, or even a *Lem* himself, may be able to take a poor girl and thus avoid paying a high price for at least one of his wives.

Lamet villages average about fifteen houses and sixty people, though they vary widely. Each village has a central community house, and the activities held in this big building help to give the community members a common interest. The community house has a special place set aside for sacrifices and for the village drum and grindstone. The equipment of the village smithy is also kept there: an anvil and blower, that the few men who know how to work iron use to repair and reforge the big machete-like Lamet knives. Twice a year, once before the sowing begins in the fields and once during the growing season, village ceremonies are held in the community house.

But this building is, first of all, a gathering place for the men of the village. They can go there to cook their favorite foods. They sit and work on baskets, crossbows, arrows, musical instruments, and all the many implements of daily life, for many of these must not be manufactured or stored in the houses. The materials from which these objects are made, as well as the finished objects themselves, are often stored in the community house, but each man keeps his things in a separate place for the use of a common building does not imply community ownership of the objects within it. When a hunter brings in game, he takes it to the community house, where one portion is cooked and eaten. The rest is distributed among the men of the village, each of whom gets at least a small piece. The skulls of the animals are placed under the roof of the community house, and though this space gradually fills with trophies the men never forget who killed which animal.

Unmarried boys, unless they are spending the night with a sweetheart, sleep in the community house, for it is considered shameful for a youth to sleep in his parents' house.

In addition to their families and their villages, the Lamet organize themselves into one other important type of group: the patrilineal clans of which there are seven. Each clan is named for a plant or animal, and no one is allowed to eat the totem species of his own clan. The members of a clan are considered to be related, no matter how distantly, and they are not allowed to intermarry. Every village must include members of at least two clans, and most villages have more. The households in any one village which belong to the same clan are usually quite closely related to one another, so that the core of the village is composed of two groups of related households, each group belonging to a different clan. But households move about so freely that most villages also include a few others as well.

All Lamets are, above all, farmers. No one spends more than a fraction of his time on any other occupation, but a few men do have special positions within the village. The man who comes closest to being the village headman is called the *xumia*. Each village has one *xumia* who must perform sacrifices to the village spirits and make sure they are not disturbed by too much disorder. The *xumia* supervises the community house and its activities and he fixes the day for village ceremonies. The importance of the spirits to which he sacrifices gives the *xumia* a certain influence in the village and he must be consulted about most activities; but the *xumia*'s authority varies with his personality and with his wealth. His suggestions are followed in ritual affairs, but if a *xumia* tries to exercise authority in other spheres without also possessing enough wealth to back up his authority, he will be ignored. The office is hereditary in the male line, and if a man should have no sons, his brother's son will inherit the office.

Each village also usually includes a man who knows how to determine which spirit is the cause of sickness and who can trace lost souls when they wander away from their bodies. This medicine man acts as a physician in performing sacrifices for the spirits which cause disease, but this function gives him no other power or rank in the village, and he is not paid for his services.

Beyond the medicine man and the *xumia,* the village has no specialists at all. Some men become a bit more skillful than others in making baskets and traps and a few know more about ironworking, but no man is totally ignorant of those crafts. Because everyone produces the same goods, the Lamets have little occasion to trade among themselves, but they do trade with other tribes. In the month after the harvest they go down to the markets along the Mekong River to sell rice and jungle products, deer hides, honey and bees' wax, baskets, a type of rice brandy, and sometimes fermented tea leaves. The horns and dried gall bladders of deer can be sold to Chinese who use them for drugs. In return the Lamets obtain iron tools, cloth, pottery, and—whenever possible—such luxuries as second-hand felt hats, glass bottles, cigar lighters, and cotton blankets. So the Lamets, like the Garos, are dependent upon markets and, through these markets, have long had access to the products and ideas of the world beyond their borders.

Tribal Peoples

The Garos and the Lamets, both in their similarities and in their differences, illustrate much about the hill people of Southeast Asia. From southern Vietnam to northern Assam, most of the hill peoples live by shifting cultivation, and everywhere the pattern of their agriculture is set by the annual cycle of the seasons. Where the weather is drier than average and the forests are cut, the soil sometimes becomes so depleted that crops no longer grow well and the possibilities for agriculture may be seriously undermined, but in most places the rain and the fertility of the soil are sufficient to allow the land to be used again after a few fallow years. In a few places, such as parts of the Shan states in Burma, the fields are used more continuously and as often for specialized crops as for rice. The Palaung of the northern Shan states, for instance, grow little except tea, which they then sell to buy rice. The Khasis in Assam now produce large quantities of potatoes for export, and a few of the Nagas on the Assam-Burma border grow more root crops than rice. The Angami Nagas even terrace their hillsides and grow wet rice, though in most other ways they have remained true to the traditions of the hills.

So the pattern of agriculture varies from tribe to tribe, depending partly upon the opportunities of the locality and partly upon the traditions of the people, but however varied its crops, each group depends upon trade with its neighbors—both the other hill tribes and the people living in the plains below—and even the few who grow little rice themselves usually look upon rice as the most desirable staple food. As settled political conditions allow people to trade more peacefully with their neighbors, each tribe will be able to concentrate on the particular crops that grow best in its own territory, and the economies of the tribal peoples are likely to become increasingly bound up with those of the dominant populations of their countries. The unique climate, terrain, and soil of their homelands could become an asset best exploited by the production of specialized crops, though at the same time the hill people would lose the subsistence basis of their former independence.

Only rarely in the past did more than a few neighboring villages maintain any effective truce. Each tribe, each valley—even each village—was more often in a state of mutual warfare with its neighbors. Often, as in the Naga Hills, this warfare took the form of headhunting raids, and in many tribes a young man had to prove himself by taking a head before he could hope to marry. Nagas, like Garos, used to display their captured human heads or skulls just as they still display the skulls of other animals. Man was considered the most dangerous and most valuable game. Nagas always conducted a ceremony when they brought home a head; in fact the killing of a human was regarded as the most effective of sacrifices in helping to ward off disease. Human flesh placed in the fields was believed to assure a good crop. Almost any human head—man, woman, or child—was acceptable, though Angami Nagas did draw the line at children who had not yet cut their first teeth. Successful headhunters were allowed to wear special clothing and ornaments.

Because it was so important to kill, the Konyak Nagas are said to have bound a captive and allowed the chief's son to hack at the helpless victim with a knife so that the boy could assume the status and symbols of a successful killer without running the risks. The killing of humans was so highly regarded that, in the early days of the British occupation of the Naga hills, men from the settled areas where headhunting was no longer possible were eager to join British-led expeditions to the unsettled country farther east. Porters on such expeditions would sometimes smuggle home an ear or a toe of a dead warrior and, even though they had not killed him, they would perform the ceremonies of the returning headhunters—a poor substitute for the glorious old days, perhaps, but better than nothing.*

Most Naga violence seems to have been carried out by small raiding parties upon unsuspecting victims. Occasionally larger war parties would face each other at a prearranged time and place, halting a spear's throw apart. They would argue, abuse one another, and then begin throwing a few stones. Eventually someone would hurl a spear, and soon a few of the more timid souls would run. Finally, one side or the other would panic and take to its heels. The result was a war with much noise but few serious casualties.

The danger of losing one's head was serious enough, however, so that villages were usually carefully guarded. Wooden or even stone fortifications were built, and sharpened splints of bamboo were hidden in the ground beneath the brush so as to make the advance of a barefoot attacker exceedingly difficult. Prisoners might be killed, but women were often kept as slaves. Slaves could be bought and

---

* The story is told of the educated Naga clerk on such an expedition who, having failed to provide himself with a spear, was seen wildly plunging the tip of his umbrella into the wounds of a fallen enemy.

sold, but they—or at least their children—gradually became incorporated into the village and joined to others by ties of kinship
until their slaves status was forgotten.

Warfare and headhunting kept most of the hill people from developing any widespread political ties, but they did not rule out a
complex internal social organization. The Lamet system is typical
of that of many tribes. Some tribes have several precisely defined
ranks rather then the two recognized by the Lamets, but social
ascent is usually accomplished by providing ample feasts for one's
neighbors and fellow villagers, and in the past was sometimes
helped by successful headhunting. With each boost in rank a man
often acquires the right to increasingly more elaborate insignia—a
special type of clothing or a special decoration on his house. The
ranks are not usually hereditary, except that the son of a rich man
may have the advantage of inheriting enough wealth to make a
good start up the social ladder. The details of the ranking system
differ from tribe to tribe, and a few tribes completely lack such a
system, but from Assam to Laos—especially among the tribes having
the least contact with the plains people—the general features of
the pattern repeat themselves. It is a system quite different from that
found among the plains people. In one way the hill system is more
open, for it is probably less difficult for a humble man to aspire to
the higher ranks, though the formality by which a series of ranks is
designated is often far more explicit than in the plains.

The hill people symbolize their own heterogeneity in a number
of ways. In clinging to their differences they seem to stand for an
ideal that is the very opposite of the American "melting pot" ideal.
This is one part of the world where the uniformity of Western
clothing has not yet displaced the excitement of local variability, and
each tribe still stubbornly continues to wear its own distinctive dress.
Many tribes are distinguished from others by the dominant color of
their clothing: the Red Karen and the Black Karen, the White Thai
and the Black Thai. Today, when settled political conditions allow
the people to mix freely, a visit to a hill market provides a spectacle
of diverse colors and styles. The women of some tribes knot their
hair over their foreheads; others, at the back. The men of some
tribes wear their hair long; others cut it close to the scalp. Silver
necklaces, bracelets, anklets, and ear ornaments are often plentiful

but the styles indicate tribal affiliation. Many of the famous Padaung women of the Burma-Thailand border still wear so many coils of brass around their necks that their necks are permanently stretched, and it is said that they can never remove the rings because they have lost the ability to hold up their heads unaided. All this diversity in styles can be understood only as a symbol of tribal affiliation—an announcement to the world that the wearer belongs to a certain tribe. The same symbolic diversity may be found in the style of houses. Bamboo predominates as a construction material, but the particular style is often typical of the tribe. Some tribes build houses of wooden planks, though their climatic and technical resources are no different from those of their neighbors. In much the same way, language seems to have come to symbolize social affiliations, and people often cling tenaciously to their distinctive language as the most prized symbol of their own tribal identity.

As a result, a traveler through the hills cannot help but be struck by the incredible variety. Each tribe has its own language, costume, architecture, and sometimes its own specialized crops. It would be a mistake, however, to conclude that each tribe has always been independent, or that each has a separate and distinct history stretching back through the centuries. It is not unreasonable to compare the tribes of the Southeast Asian hills to the Christian denominations of the United States. Like the Southeast Asian tribes, each Christian denomination has its separate tradition and historical development. People often take their own denomination seriously, demonstrate their adherence to it in a variety of symbolic ways (though not quite so obviously as Southeast Asians display their tribal affiliations), and—with greater frequency than could be expected by chance alone—marry within their own group. Yet people sometimes change their denominations and, however separate one denomination may be from another today, the members of one cannot realistically be understood as having descended in isolation from those of all others. In the same way, the members of Southeast Asian tribes must have regularly mixed and even switched affiliations. It is rare today for tribal people to be particularly fussy about intermarriage, for instance, so regular genetic intermixture has taken place and the intermixture of customs has surely followed.

Nevertheless, the tendency for neighbors to copy each other's behavior has never outstripped the tendency toward variety, and in one other respect the hill people are far more diverse than the people of the plains: family organization. Most plains people have families rather reminiscent of those of Europe or America, but almost any kind of family and kinship organization that one can imagine can be found somewhere in the hills. A few tribes, like the Garo take their name, clan affiliation, and inheritance from their mothers, while others, like the Lamet, have a patrilineal system. Still others have less marked emphasis on either side. Perhaps the historical absence of settled government in the hills forced the people into greater dependence upon their kinsmen and encouraged them to form elaborate groups, such as lineages and clans, upon which they could count for support. One can find among one's kinsmen the most reliable source of help in a dispute and support in battle. The particular ways in which one can organize the support of kinsmen are endless but, to some degree at least, they can all be seen as helping to satisfy the human need for mutual protection and defense. In the plains, the centralized governments provided protection in a different way, and to that extent helped to reduce the importance of kinship.

Compared with the people of the more densely populated plains, the hill people are relatively few in number, but their variety is much greater and their territory larger. If not ignored by the plains people, they are often looked upon as rustic and backward, and they in turn regard the plains people with both anger and contempt as sophisticated and powerful scoundrels. Yet the peoples of the hills and of the plains have much in common, and one can at least speculate that the cultural traits still so widespread in the hills were once characteristic of the plains as well. It is now many centuries since the people of the plains began to fuse into the civilizations of Southeast Asia. Nobody can now determine with any certainty what the plains were like before this fusion began, but conceivably the people of the plains were once not so different from the hill tribes of more recent centuries.

Chapter Five

The Hinduized Kingdoms

○

The Indian Influence

Two thousand years ago the lowland plains of mainland Southeast Asia were probably already occupied by farmers who grew wet rice as their staple crop and raised domesticated dogs, pigs, chickens, buffalo, and cattle. They certainly used metal objects and probably had at least a rudimentary knowledge of both bronze and iron metallurgy. They probably made extensive use of boats on the many rivers which wind through the lowland areas. To judge by the widespread distribution of recent customs, it is a good guess that most of the people lived in small households formed around a single married couple and their children, and that they believed themselves to be surrounded by spirits who needed to be treated with care and respect lest they bring disease and bad luck. Their agriculture may have been productive enough to support a reasonably dense population, and no doubt there were locally important chiefs, but there is no evidence that they ever built settlements larger than an agricultural village. There are no cities, no remains of art or sculpture, no evidence of writing or of the philosophical systems which characterized the later peoples. All these were to come from India and to form an amalgam with the indigenous customs. The kingdoms that arose can only be understood as representing a fusion of local and foreign traits: the basic subsistence techniques, family forms, and views of the world must have been indigenous; the writing, philosophical religions, and conceptions of royalty were originally foreign. The foreign and the indigenous gradually came to blend together intimately, and ever since, the blend has characterized the kingdoms which have been found in Southeast Asia.

Trade between India and Southeast Asia may well have begun in prehistoric times, but contact quickened in the first few centuries of

64

the Christian era, and from that time onward the evidence of Indian influence grows increasingly strong. Curiously, the earliest evidence comes neither from India nor from Southeast Asia, but from Europe and China. The first hints seem to be *Periplus of the Erythran Sea,* a Greek account of trade and seafaring which dates from about 70 A.D. After mentioning the ports of western India, this account refers to other, still more distant ports to which Indian ships sailed. An island known as Chryse was said to produce tortoise shell, and as tortoise shell has been a product of the Indonesian archipelago, Chryse or "Gold Island" has been taken to refer to Sumatra, though the name of "Gold Land" was later applied to Burma as well. In the middle of the second century. the Alexandrian geographer, Ptolemy, gave a less vague description, and maps regarded as copies of Ptolemy's original show the coast of Burma and even the Malay peninsula quite clearly. He described "Silver Land" and "Gold Land" which were near the towns of the "Golden Peninsula," the "Chryse Chersonesus." He also mentions various islands, presumably of the archipelago, most of which he claimed were inhabited either by cannibals or by men with tails. Ptolemy must have learned of these countries indirectly from Indians, for he uses proper names in their Indian form, but the Indians themselves left hardly any historical records from such an early date.

For more than vague references to early Southeast Asia, one must turn to China. Chinese travelers, sometimes officials on diplomatic visits, sometimes pilgrims on their way to Buddhist centers in India, wrote of the countries they had seen. The picture drawn by their reports is one of Indianized kingdoms in most of the lowland areas on the periphery of the mainland and in Sumatra and Java as well. These were both commercial centers and centers of Indianized art, royalty, and religion, and it was from these centers that Indian influences gradually radiated to the countryside.

Several motives probably lay behind the migration and settlement of Indians. Both India and China were building more seaworthy ships, so that long voyages were not quite so dangerous as they had been. In the west, European ship captains learned to exploit the monsoon and although the Arabs had possessed this knowledge earlier, its spread no doubt helped to stimulate trade between Europe and India, and this in turn had repercussions on the trade further east. The new Indianized states lay near the eastern end of the famous spice route that passed through Southeast Asia to India and Arabia and, finally, to Europe. As European commerce increased during the time of the Roman Empire, the demand for imports stimulated trade all the way eastward. Not all the trade was for spices; both India and Europe sought sandalwood and other aromatic woods. India received great quantities of gold from the Roman Empire, and when Rome finally tried to stop the outward flow of gold, Indian traders may have turned to Southeast Asia as an alternate source. In later centuries cloth was India's most important export to Southeast Asia, and the beginnings of the cloth trade may well date from this time.

Another factor encouraging Indian migration may have been Buddhism, which was then a vital force in India. The Buddha had opposed the strict caste system and his teachings may have freed some Indians from the ideas of ritual purity which are so important in Hinduism and made it easier for them to travel and settle in foreign lands, and even to take foreign wives. In some parts of Southeast Asia, the very earliest evidences of Indian contact are images of the Buddha.

As a result of these forces, and perhaps of others which can no longer be reconstructed, Indians began to settle in the coastal communities of Southeast Asia. Originally following ancient trade routes, their numbers gradually increased. Most of them must have been traders who exchanged Indian goods for local products, but the merchants were soon joined by teachers, and priests who effectively transmitted Indian ideology and Indian religion. Royal lines were established which claimed descent from Indian forebears and which used Indian rituals to validate their claim.

It has sometimes been supposed that Indian warriors or adventurers actually conquered territory in Southeast Asia and set themselves up as local rulers. Had they done so, they would have used their own Indian language and ritual in the courts, but they would have had to learn the local language and adapt to local customs in order to deal with their subjects. However, the results would have been much the same if, as seems more likely, local chiefs who witnessed from afar the splendor of India seized upon some of the symbols of Indian royalty in an attempt to enhance their own position. They could have imported priests from India to provide them with glamorous rituals and to validate their claims to royalty in accordance with the classical Hindu and Buddhist writings. The priests would naturally use Indian languages in their religious and royal rituals. The local chiefs, now converted into kings, would welcome traders from India who would bring profit to the kingdoms, and Indian ideas could grow strong at the courts even without military conquest or an abrupt break with the past.

The ordinary farmer kept right on planting his rice, worshipping his spirits, and raising his children according to his own traditions. Even in the capital towns the bulk of the population probably always followed indigenous customs. Certainly the local languages continued in use everywhere, for in spite of their great prestige in rituals, the Indian languages never threatened to become established among the common people. The caste system, the assignment of occupation by birth, and the Indian concept of ritual purity never took hold. Most of the immigrants were probably single men, and if they married local women their wives could not help them to pass on the rules of caste, and their children would first learn the local language. Even a Hindu immigrant would have found it difficult to insist that his children maintain the caste purity he had ignored by marrying a local woman.

Nevertheless, if much that is fundamental in Indian culture failed to take hold, other traits of equal importance became firmly established. Most of these concerned palace life, and for many centuries the main channel for Indian ideas was through the courts and through the towns in which they were established. Nothing that came from India was more important than religion. Buddhism was certainly present from the earliest times as can be seen by the early appearance of Buddha images. The first figures are in the style distinctive of Amaravati, a center of a school of Buddhist sculpture located eighty miles from the east coast of central India. Amaravati flourished in the second and third centuries, and this helps to fix the time and source of Indian contacts. Perhaps Buddhism was the most important religious force among individual immigrants, but the new states were soon to adopt the Shivaite-Hindu concept of royalty. In return for lofty rituals and impressive genealogies, the kings granted their patronage to their Brahman priests. As a result, the ritual which has surrounded—and still surrounds—the royalty of Southeast Asia has been largely Brahmanic. Moreover, the philosophical conception of state and king derived directly from India. Where Hindu ideas were strongest, the king was considered to be an incarnation of a god or a descendant of one of the Hindu deities, Shiva or Vishnu. Later, when Buddhism became dominant, this view was modified, but even then the king's position in the world was considered to parallel the position of an important deity in the cosmos. The palace became the earthly equivalent of the celestial mountain believed to occupy the center of the universe. Many kings assumed the title "King of the Mountain," and built their palaces and religious buildings on the peaks of hills. The symbolic association between the palace and the celestial mountain meant that the palace itself assumed great significance, and physical possession of the palace was sometimes enough to validate the position of the king in the eyes of his subjects. A ruler was sometimes afraid to leave his palace for fear that in his absence a rival would seize it and declare himself king. Certain sacred laws of Hinduism, the Dharmashastras, and particularly the so-called Laws of Manu, as taught by the Brahmans, became important.

Buddhism, Shivaite Hinduism, and a bit later the cult of Vishnu, all found their way into Southeast Asia, and it is often difficult to make a clear distinction among them, however clearly distinguishable Buddhism and Hinduism are today. Tantric Buddhism, one of the earliest forms of Buddhism to be important in Southeast Asia, showed marked Hindu features, and Hindus tended to accept Buddhism as another Hindu cult.

With religion came sacred languages. The first of these was Sanskrit, the language of the sacred texts of Hinduism and of certain schools of Buddhism. The Sanskrit scripts are the first form of writing known to have reached Southeast Asia. These scripts were alphabetic, but entirely different from the alphabets of Europe. Each consonant was symbolized by a distinctive letter, but the following vowel was indicated by the choice of accents, hooks, and curlicues placed in front, behind, above, or below the consonant. In the alphabet itself, the consonants were arranged according to the sounds they represented, (for instance, all the letters for sounds made by closing the lips together were grouped together). The Sanskrit alphabet was the first of this sort, and examples can still be seen in rock inscriptions scattered widely over Southeast Asia, but similar alphabets were soon adapted to the local languages as well. The form of the letters was modified, though not beyond recognition, but the order of the letters was generally retained. Enough changes had to be made to cope with sounds not found in the Indian languages. In Burmese, for instance, special marks were added to show whether the syllable was to be spoken in a high tone or a low one, but for all their local variety and adaptation, the alphabets used today for the Burmese, Thai, Laotian, and Cambodian languages all derive originally from Indian prototypes.

The local languages lacked not only a script, but also words for the philosophical, religious, and legal concepts which came from India. As a result, hundreds of words of Indian origin were borrowed by local languages just as Latin and French terms have been borrowed by English. The calendar used in most of the mainland countries is based directly upon Indian models. It is a lunar calendar which recognizes a cycle of twelve months, each of which begins with a new moon. Since the solar year contains roughly twelve and one third lunar months, a thirteenth month is inserted into the calendar about every three years, much as the European calendar inserts an extra day each leap year to keep in step with astronomical events. Also adopted was the Indian seven-day week, with each day named for a deity and associated with one of the seven wandering heavenly bodies. This imported calendar has regulated the ceremonial cycle, and it has also been widely used for astrological calculations. Southeast Asians have taken the motions of the heavenly bodies very seriously as prognostications of the future. Every Burmese child is provided with an inscription which states the exact moment of his birth, so that astrologers will be able to foretell his future with precision, and the Burmese chose 3:40 A.M. on January 4, 1948, as the moment to gain their formal independence from Britain because the arrangement of the planets at that time was judged to be auspicious.

Indian literature and Indian mythology have delighted generations of Southeast Asians. Puppet shows, shadow plays, and live dramatic performances based on the tales of the Ramayana have been popular everywhere. The Indian epics, the Puranas, and the Jataka tales have all been taken over. The art and sculpture of Southeast Asia have utilized themes from Indian literature, and their forms clearly show the influence of Indian style.

Although the Indian caste system was not adopted, the class system which developed among the lowland people of Southeast Asia grew out of the social setting of the courts and their capital towns. Wherever Indian influence was strong, a division grew up between the farming majority and the ruling aristocracy. The kings and their relatives and courtiers were set off from the rest of the population by custom, speech, style of life, and by insignia of rank and office. The aristocracy has been more or less hereditary, but never as rigidly so as in India. Intermarriage between the classes has never been completely prohibited. Commoners have sometimes been able to rise into the aristocracy, and from time to time commoners have even managed to fight their way to become kings, though after having done so they have consistently provided themselves with elaborate if mythical genealogies to validate their position. Members of the royalty could also slip down the social scale. One of the kings' prerogatives has been to have many wives and consorts, and as a result they have had great numbers of children. It has hardly been feasible for all these descendants to have the same degree of royal importance, so that each succeeding generation was systematically lower in rank than its more royal predecessors, until finally the descendants fell back into the commoner class.

Early Customs: The Historical Records

Unfortunately, only little is known of the daily life of the early kingdoms and almost nothing is known of life in the countryside. What little knowledge is available has been gleaned from Chinese records. The earliest of these refer to a kingdom called "Funan," located in what is now Cambodia, and report that the kingdom was founded in the first century A.D., although the records themselves date from two centuries later. In A.D. 243, Funan sent an embassy to China (on what today would be called a good-will mission) which included musicians and products of the country, and a few years later the Chinese sent a mission back to Funan. A member of this expedition, a man named K'ang T'ai, provided the first eyewitness account of any Southeast Asian kingdom.

According to K'ang T'ai, Funan had been founded by a foreigner named Kaundinya who was guided to the site of his future kingdom by knowledge revealed in a dream. His victory was made possible by a magic arrow which he used to attack the defending queen's boat, but afterwards he married the queen and founded the dynasty which ruled for the next one-hundred-fifty years. (Other, more detailed versions of this story have Kaundinya throwing a sacred javelin to mark the site of his capital and then marrying Soma, the daughter of the king of the *nagas*. *Nagas* are giant serpents—reminiscent both of dragons and cobras—and they have figured largely in Southeast Asian mythology. The myth of the marriage between a conquering king and a *naga* princess was part of the heritage that Funan acquired from India and passed on to later kingdoms.)

K'ang T'ai also commented briefly on the customs of the country:

> There are walled towns, palaces and living houses. The men are ugly and black, their hair is frizzly; they go naked, are barefoot. Their character is simple, and they are free of thievery. They are given to agriculture. They sow one year and harvest for three, and they like to engrave ornaments and to work with a chisel. Many of the utensils which they use for eating are of silver. A tax is paid on gold, silver, pearls, and perfumes. They have books, and archives, and other things. Their written characters resemble those of the Hou.[1]

After the middle of the fourth century, Sanskrit inscriptions help to determine the location and chronologies of the kingdoms, but most of the details continue to come from Chinese records. The history of the southern Chi dynasty gives a somewhat fuller account of Funan.[2] This history must have been assembled uncritically from several sources for it first describes the people as "evil and cunning" men who captured the inhabitants of neighboring cities and enslaved them. Only a few lines later, however, it says that the inhabitants were of good character and that they did not like war although they were invaded without respite by their neighbors. The merchandise of Funan was described as including gold, silver, and silk, and the people made rings and bracelets of gold and vessels of silver. The sons of the great families wore brocade sarongs, the women wore cloth around their heads, and even the poor people covered themselves with pieces of cloth. Their houses were built of wood, raised off the ground (probably on piles) and enclosed within wooden palisades, and the king lived in a many-storied pavilion. A "great bamboo" grew by the sea, and the people wove its leaves, which were eight or nine feet long, and used them to cover their houses. They also made boats eight or nine *tchang* long (a *tchang* is about ten feet) and as much as six or seven *tchang* wide. The bow and stern of the boats were shaped like the head and tail of a fish. For amusement, the people watched cock fights and pig fights. They had no prisons, but if a legal contest arose, gold rings or eggs were thrown into boiling water, and the contending parties had to retrieve them. According to the Chi history, the hands of the guilty man would be completely scorched, but those of the innocent would be uninjured.

A somewhat later text adds a few more details.[3] The people of Funan did not dig wells, but several dozen families would share a common basin from which they drew water. They worshipped the spirits of the sky and had bronze images of these beings. Some images had two faces and four arms; others had four faces and eight arms. Each hand held something—a child, a bird, or animal, the sun, or the moon. When the king went traveling, he rode on an elephant, as did his concubines and courtiers.

It was customary to shave the beard and head as a sign of mourning, and there were four types of burial: burial in water (which consisted of throwing the corpse into a fast-flowing river); burial by fire (which consisted of cremating the corpse); burial in the earth; and burial "by birds" (which consisted of abandoning the corpse in the open countryside).

Funan was the first of the great states of Southeast Asia and for five centuries it was the dominant power on the mainland. Even after its power declined in the sixth century, its prestige endured and the rulers of the later kingdoms invoked the memory of Funan to enhance their own reigns. The legends of the sacred mountain and of the *naga* princess were taken over by the kings of Cambodia, and the roots of some of the great artistic and architectural traditions of Cambodia may be in those of Funan. Indeed, when Funan declined, the bulk of the population must have remained to father the people of later kingdoms. Although some migration surely occurred, Funan—in a sense—did not die at all; it was simply replaced by later kingdoms which built upon the same traditions.

Champa (or Lin-yi, as the Chinese first called it) was situated to the north and east of Funan, in what is now South Vietnam. It may have been founded within a century or so of Funan and it shared many of the same customs. Champa first entered history when it came into conflict with the southernmost wing of the Chinese imperial power which had already become established in what is now North Vietnam, For many hundreds of years the people of Champa fought with and gradually lost ground to the Sinicised Vietnamese, but they held out as a separate power until the fourteenth century when their country was finally absorbed by Vietnam.

Shortly before 600 A.D., a Chinese visitor to Champa reported that the inhabitants built their houses of fired bricks covered with a layer of lime. Both men and women wore only a piece of cloth wrapped around the body. They pierced their ears, and wore little rings in them. The elite wore leather footwear, but commoners went barefoot. The king wore an elaborate headgear ornamented with golden flowers and a tuft of silk. Like the kings of Funan, he traveled on an elephant. On his journeys he was sheltered by a parasol, preceded by drummers and by men blowing conch shells, and surrounded by servants. (Even today, the right to use parasols of various colors, sizes, and shapes remains a symbol of certain political or spiritual statuses.)

Marriage in ancient Champa always took place during the eighth moon, the time of the monsoon. Marriage proposals were initiated by the girls because, the Chinese observer reported, they were considered to be inferior by nature. Couples with the same family name were not forbidden to marry, a custom which seemed strange to the Chinese visitor.

The report goes on to say that the people had a bellicose and cruel character. For weapons they had bows and arrows, swords, lances, and crossbows of bamboo. Their musical instruments resembled those of China, such as the cithern, the five-string violin, and the flute. Conch shells and drums were used to warn the people of approaching danger. To the Chinese, the people seemed to have deep-set eyes, straight jutting noses, black and curly hair. The women tied their hair on the top of their heads in the shape of a hammer. The funeral of the king took place seven days after his death; that of a high mandarin, after three days; and that of a commoner, on the very next day. Whatever the mode of death, the body was carefully wrapped, and—accompanied by drums and dancers—was carried to the edge of the sea or river and cremated there. Whatever fragments of bones then remained were gathered from the ashes. The bones of a king were placed in a golden urn and thrown in the sea; those of a high official were enclosed in a silver urn and thrown into the mouth of a river; those of one who had enjoyed no distinction in life were put in an earthen vase which was received by the waters of a river. The funeral procession was followed by relatives of both sexes, who cut their hair before reaching the river. (This was the only sign of a very short mourning period.) Some widows, however, remained in mourning throughout their lives and would show this by letting their hair straggle loosely after it had grown in again. These were women who had renounced remarriage forever, a custom which sounds more typical of India than of Southeast Asia.[4]

Chinese reports from the Menam and Irrawady basins to the west are less detailed. These areas are farther from China and were less likely to be visited by Chinese travelers, but as they are closer to India, Indian influence could have been even earlier and stronger than in Funan. Unfortunately, archaeological and epigraphical evidence is scanty, but the lack of evidence does not prove that Hinduized kingdoms did not develop as early in the west as in the east. The earliest inscriptions in central Burma date from about 500 A.D., and give the first hints of a little-known people, the Pyu. Legends trace the Pyu back many centuries earlier, but these tales can be accepted only with caution. The earliest remains of the Mon, a people once spread widely over southern Burma, go back no earlier than 500 A.D., and a kingdom known as Dvaravati, also presumably Mon in speech, flourished in the Menam basin (now central Thailand), in the seventh century. Their antecedents may be as early as those of Funan and Champa, but the evidence is lacking. The most famous of the Hinduized states is certainly that of the

Khmer of Cambodia. After the seventh century, the Khmer kingdom gradually rose to replace Funan, and its capital at Angkor was founded in the latter part of the ninth century. In the course of the next few hundred years the capital was to become a monumental center which ranks as one of the great architectural and artistic masterpieces of the world. Angkor remained the capital of the Khmer until 1432, when it was abandoned; two years later the present capital of Phnom Penh was founded. The modern Cambodians are the direct descendants of the builders of Angkor. In spite of the attempts of various Europeans to glamorize their "discoveries," Angkor—though abandoned and left to the encroachment of the jungle—had never really been lost or forgotten. Today the ruins of Angkor have been partially restored, and every year they attract thousands of visitors.

The buildings which compose Angkor are scattered over several square miles. The largest, Angkor Wat, is surrounded by a square moat almost a mile long on each side within which are a series of square enclosures, increasing in height toward the center. Towers adorn the corners of the enclosures, and at the center a sanctuary rises one hundred and thirty feet above the forty-foot terrace on which it stands. Originally the towers were covered with gold, and the central shrine contained a statue of Vishnu. The gold and the statue are now gone, but the entire outer wall of the sanctuary is still covered with sculptures in relief. Thousands of figures—animals and gods, kings and commoners, soldiers and civilians—adorn the walls, and many of the features of ancient Cambodian life can still be seen in the scenes depicted. A few miles from Angkor Wat is the Bayon, less well preserved but equally impressive with its great stone towers carved with faces directed toward the four points of the compass. Many other ruins are found nearby, some are crumbling and covered with jungle growth, but their carvings and general form still testify to the superlative skill and artistic feeling of the builders of Angkor.

Only one eyewitness account of the flourishing period of Angkor has been preserved. It, too, was written by a Chinese—one Chou Ta-kuan, who visited the capital as a member of a Chinese embassy in 1296. Fortunately, his account was a full one. After describing the layout of the city, he went on to say something of the customs of the people. The governmental bureaucracy must have been complex, for Chou Ta-kuan describes councilors, generals, astronomers, and all types of petty officials down to the police officers found in each village. The officeholders were generally princes, but a commoner might also be selected to hold a high office. If so, he generally gave his daughter as a royal concubine. The official rank of each person was reflected in his house and his clothing, and one important symbol of rank was the right to use a parasol of a particular size and of a specified number of tiers.

The people used a seven-day week, and although they did not have family names, their personal names were based on the name of the day of their birth (a practice like that still found in Burma). Disputes were arbitrated by the king, and truthfulness was tested by a variety of ordeals. Those proven guilty were punished by having their fingers, toes, or arms amputated, or even by being buried alive. Debauchery and gambling, however, were not forbidden. The people were said to be boorish and very dark. Both men and women wore their hair tied in a knot at the nape of the neck. They had many qualities of cloth, some woven locally, some imported from Thailand or from Champa and the most highly valued cloth came from "the west" (presumably India). The king wore gaudy jewelry and fancy cloth, and although he went barefoot, the soles of his feet and the palms of his hands were stained red. Among the common people, only the women stained their soles and palms. Commoners wore only a bit of cloth about their loins, and both men and women left their chests uncovered.

There seems already to have been a distinction between plains people and hill people, for Chou reported that the people of Angkor purchased savages who came from the mountains to work as servants. They were a race apart and did not mix with the other people. He reported that all girls underwent a defloration ceremony performed by a Buddhist or "Taoist" (presumably Hindu) priest, but Chou admitted that he did not learn for certain whether this was done by hand or, as he had heard it claimed, through intercourse with the priest. The women, he was told, were very lustful, and if their husbands remained away on business, they were unable to stay alone for many nights. Many men married women who had first been their mistresses, and the Chinese visitor seemed surprised to note that this was a subject of neither shame nor of astonishment.

Chou also remarked on the rapidity with which women recovered from childbirth:

> After giving birth to a child, a woman cooks rice, rolls it in salt, and applies it to the sexual parts. After a day and a night she removes it. Thereby the pregnancy has no unfortunate aftereffects, and the woman keeps the appearance of a young girl. In the family where I was lodging a girl bore a child, and I was able thus to inform myself. The next day, bearing her child in her arms, she went with him to bathe in the river. It is really extraordinary.[5]

The dead were disposed of by being left exposed to birds of prey. This custom was long admired, and as late as 1859 the Cambodian king demonstrated his Buddhist piety by having his flesh fed in morsels to birds of prey.

Chou identified several types of religious leaders and officials. First were scholars, whom he called *pan-k'i*. They were not organized into temples or associations; nor were they distinguished by dress, except that they tied a cord of white thread about their necks. In India the white thread marks a man of high caste, so presumably these *pan-k'i* were Brahmans. Priests of another type, called *tch'ou-kou* by the Chinese visitor, wore yellow skirts and an upper garment which left the right shoulder uncovered. They shaved their heads and went barefoot. Clearly the *tch'ou-kou* were Buddhist monks. They were associated with temples in which images of the Buddha were kept. These monks ate fish and meat, but they did not drink wine. They recited texts inscribed on palm leaves and sometimes gave instruction to children of the laity. This account given by Chou could be a description of the Buddhist monks who follow the southern school of Buddhism in Southeast Asia today.

Chou mentioned still another group of religious men. These were the *pa-sseu-wei*, who were probably Shivaite Hindus. They dressed like laymen except that they tied a bit of red or white cloth around their heads. Their temples were smaller than those of the Buddhists. The *pa-sseu-wei* did not share food with other men, nor did they eat in public or drink wine. Religion seems to have played an important role in Cambodia and one of Chou's few remarks about the villages is that each one had a temple or stupa.

The early kingdoms fostered the development of two social classes —a distinction which endured through the colonial period and colors the social relationships within these countries even today. The lives of the farmers were limited to their villages, their padi fields, and their families, and their relationships with one another were regulated by mutual and communal obligations. Giving symbolic order and importance to their world, however, was the capital city, the symbol of the city of heaven. Its aristocracy was wealthy and acquisitive, treasuring refined and graceful manners but operating in an atmosphere of intrigue and rivalry which contrasted sharply with village life. But aristocrat and commoner alike accepted the fundamental order of the universe, and each unquestioningly granted the place of the other within it. Empires and dynasties rose and fell. Invaders conquered and wars were fought, yet this fundamental order survived and prevailed. Of course, changes have come, and some of these will be considered, but life in Southeast Asia still reflects the time when the civilization of India was first carried eastward.

Notes

1. Paul Pelliot, "Le Fou-nan," *Bulletin de l'École française d'extrême-Orient*, III (1903), 254.
2. *Ibid.*, pp. 261–62.
3. *Ibid.*, pp. 263–72.
4. Le Marquis d'Hervey de Saint Denys, *Ethnographie des peuples étrangers à la Chine*, Vol. II: *Peuples méridionaux. Ouvrage composé au XIIIe siècle de notre ère, par Ma-touan-lin*, translated by Le Marquis d'Hervey de Saint-Denys (Geneva, 1883).
5. Paul Pelliot, "Mémoire sur les coutumes du Cambodge par Tcheou Ta-kouan. Traduits et annotés par P. Pelliot," *Bulletin de l'École française d'extréme-Orient*, II (1902), 123–77.

Chapter Six

Buddhism and the Burmese

The Buddha

To the casual traveler in Southeast Asia, and to the people themselves, no aspect of life seems so important as Buddhism. Throughout Burma, Thailand, and Cambodia, evidence of devotion to the Buddha is everywhere. Yellow-robed monks begging their food from the faithful laity patrol every village and every city neighborhood. Pagodas and monasteries dot the countryside.

If the civilization of Europe could ever have been fairly called "Christian," then the civilization of these countries today can surely be labeled "Buddhist," and indeed Christianity and Buddhism have curiously similar histories. Just as Christianity grew out of ancient religious traditions of the Near East and was brought to Europe by proselytizing missionaries, so Buddhism arose out of the ancient traditions of Hindu India and was carried northward and eastward to other countries. Both doctrines are traced back to a great leader and teacher who has merited the veneration of generations of followers, and both Christianity and Buddhism subsequently declined in importance in the countries of their origin—Buddhism to the point of extinction.

Having originated in India, Buddhism shares many of its most fundamental assumptions with Hinduism: the belief in the cycle of rebirth, and the belief that animals as well as men have souls. Of the many facets of Southeast Asian life influenced by India, none is so important as Buddhism. The story of Buddha's birth, life, doctrines, and death is as vital a part of the traditions of Southeast Asia as is that of Christ in the West. Every Thai and Burmese child knows at least the outline of Buddha's story. As in all such stories, it is often difficult to distinguish the historical truth from the cherished myth, but in this case the myth is surely more important. It is the myth that people repeat and believe, and it is the myth by which they try to guide their lives. It is a story that has inspired many millions.

Gautama Buddha is believed to have been born to a royal family which reigned along the northern border of India in the sixth century B.C. He was raised amid the wealth and luxury that only a royal family could provide, and a prophecy about his future led his father, the king, to shield him from any knowledge of the pain and suffering so widespread in the world. In innocence, Gautama grew to manhood and married, but at the age of twenty-nine he witnessed the four signs which showed him the true state of the world and which changed the course of his entire life: an old man, a sick man, a dead man, and a monk. Thus Gautama learned of sickness, old age, and death, and he could no longer permit himself to continue his worldly and luxurious life. He resolved to retire from the world and to seek enlightenment.

He then left his family, his wealth, and his social rank and became a monk, begging for his food from house to house. He sought teachers, placed himself under the tutelage of famed Brahmans who instructed him in the methods of meditation, and experimented with asceticism. He felt that having to beg for his food was in itself a hindrance to his ascetic practices and so he set himself an even stricter practice: first he limited himself to the fruit that had dropped by itself from trees, then to the fruit which dropped from the very tree under which he sat, then to a single fruit, then to a single grain of rice, and finally to a single sesamum seed each day. His body was emaciated; his skin lost its golden color and became dry and black. For six years he practiced this austerity, but in the end he concluded that enlightenment was not to be achieved by such extreme measures and he abandoned them.

Then one day, after eating a meal of milk and porridge, he took his noonday rest in the pleasant shade of a grove of trees on a river bank, and in the evening he went to sit under a Bo tree. As he sat, crosslegged, beneath the tree, he resolved not to stir from that spot until he had achieved supreme and absolute wisdom. An evil god tried to frighten him from his place, but the future Buddha used his power of loving kindness to win a peaceful victory over the god. During the night he successively attained the knowledge of previous existences, the divine eye with which he could see the beings of all thirty-one planes of existence, and finally the bliss of complete emancipation by which he reached supreme wisdom. This was the moment of supreme enlightenment. He had become a Buddha. Soon, the Buddha preached his first sermons, and through the rest of his long life he traveled, preached, and converted an ever-growing number of followers. In his eightieth year, surrounded by his adoring disciples, he passed away into Nirvana.

The Doctrine of the Buddha

The doctrine that the Buddha taught—or at any rate the doctrine that has been handed down as his—may at first seem harsh or even gloomy, for it is centered on the belief that suffering and pain are the outstanding traits of this world. This view is put forth in the Four Noble Truths, the central tenets of Buddhist theology:

1. The quality of existence in this world is unsatisfactory and even painful. Ceaselessly recurring illness, old age, death, and decay bring endless suffering. Why should this suffering exist?

2. The painfulness of man's existence is caused by his desires— his craving for worldly objects, even his craving for life itself. People become attached to worldly things which are, by their very nature, transitory and impermanent. How can man avoid the pain which the separation from such attachments will surely cause?

3. Man's suffering will cease only when desire itself has been banished, for the means to satisfy selfish desires can only be temporary and must in the end be painfully lost. How can man rid himself of the craving and desire for the transitory attachments of life?

4. The answer is that only by following the Buddhist path of enlightened self-discipline can man totally rid himself of selfish desires. By proper moral conduct and insight, he can reduce his desires and eventually escape completely from the passions of the world and thus end the cycle of existences in which all living beings are caught.

The path which the Buddha recommended for achieving these ends is one of righteous social behavior and careful self-discipline— behavior which Buddhists summarize as the "eightfold path": Right Views—an understanding of the Four Noble Truths and awareness of the fact that all existence is impermanent and painful; Right Intent—elimination of all lustful, evil, or cruel intentions from one's mind; Right Speech—no lying or frivolity; Right Conduct—refrainment from taking the life of any creature, from theft, and from improper sexual behavior; Right Livelihood—abstention from any occupation that might involve deception, violence, or injury to others; Right Effort—cultivation of a pure state of mind by the repression of all thoughts of wrong behavior and the development of right thoughts and behavior; Right Contemplation—contemplation of one's own body, emotions, feeling, and mind, thereby seeking to become detached from them so as to become their master; and Right Concentration—the search for the ultimate tranquility and insight through proper meditative practices.

Buddhism is a singularly intellectual creed. It is a creed that does not require faith in any supernatural realm such as is often felt to be an indispensable part of religion. The doctrine requires no gods. The Buddha denied his own divinity, and many of his followers have not regarded him as a god. To be sure, the Buddha was a very great man and a great teacher, and the stories which have arisen about his life have given it a quality quite different from that of the lives of most men, but for all that, the Buddha remained a man. He is considered to have been in his final existence and to have achieved, as few men do, the extinction of all desire. But every man may aspire to the same achievement. No heaven awaits the soul after its life on earth is past. This life will be followed by another life on earth and that by another in a long and almost endless cycle, a cycle which can be terminated only by the extinction of one's individual identity.

With no gods, there is no one toward whom prayers can be directed, and although Buddhists chant and bow low before statues of the Buddha, these are, in principle not prayers, but aids to contemplation and insight. Of course, the chants and verbal formulae that humble men recite may seem to differ little, even to the worshippers, from mechanically repeated Christian prayers, but to the truly thoughtful worshipper the difference is a profound one. With no gods and no prayer, but simply a theory of the universe and an explanation for man's sorry state, each man becomes responsible for his own salvation. Every man can meditate by himself;

he requires no church and no priest to act as an intermediary between himself and some god.

Buddhist communities do give help to anyone who desires to live according to the eightfold path. The community provides pagodas and statues of the Buddha to help inspire the proper frame of mind, to assist the worshippers in their meditation, and to allow them to achieve a fuller self-awareness. The holy orders offer a place for men and women who wish to devote themselves to their search for true understanding, but a monk is above all on a personal quest for his own salvation. Although monks are admired by the laity and respected for their austere ways and their devotion to the teachings of the Buddha, and although by accepting gifts monks give laymen the chance to gain merit, the monks are not priests, and do not stand between the individual Buddhist and the road to salvation.

Perhaps this doctrine is too rarefied to satisfy completely the needs of most people. Complex ritual, elaborate dogma, and a faith in personal but supernatural powers can shield helpless men from the terrors of their world, and no people are so thoroughly committed to this pure form of Buddhism as to reject completely all other alternate doctrines. Multitudes of spirits and gods have been worshipped and honored, tolerated along with Buddhism. Japan has had its Shinto rituals, China its Confucian doctrine and the more mystical Taoist cults, and in Southeast Asia no nation has ever tried to banish its spirits, or the lively rituals and beliefs which cluster around them. Not only has Buddhism tolerated other religions, but the various Buddhist sects have rarely persecuted each other with the enthusiasm that Christian sects have so often shown. Buddhists have not been unanimous in their theology, and indeed different interpretations of the Buddha's teachings arose in the early centuries after his death. Other schools have accumulated more supernatural doctrine than the Theravada branch found in most of Southeast Asia, but the various sects have generally been mutually tolerant.

The Spread of Buddhism

For Buddhism to succeed as a practical faith, it needed a secular champion, and it found one in the great King Asoka who governed an empire in northern India in the third century B.C. According to popular legend, this king had gone to war and, after a series of bloody battles, had successfully vanquished his enemies, only to look upon the blood of the battlefield and to be overcome with revulsion. He resolved to renounce war and henceforth to devote himself to the spread of Buddhism. It is perhaps fortunate for the faith that he waited until after his victories to make his resolution, for by that time he was a powerful king with ample resources. He erected numerous monuments, some of which still stand, and he sent missionaries to all parts of his empire and (in popular belief at least) beyond its borders as well.

No substantial evidence supports the tradition that he sent missionaries to Burma, but the traditions of Buddhist influence in Ceylon during Asoka's time may be less questionable. The king of Ceylon is said to have asked Asoka for missionaries and to have sent an embassy to India to fetch a shoot of the sacred Bo tree under which the Buddha received enlightenment. From this beginning, Ceylon was to grow into a seat of Buddhist learning, and the center in which the Theravada doctrine was codified.

As early as the fifth century A.D., the Buddhist scholars of Ceylon were codifying the sacred texts into a form known as the Pali Cannon (they are written in the Pali language), and these have remained the fundamental documents of Theravada Buddhism. How early direct contact between Ceylon and Southeast Asia was established is now impossible to say, but it may well go back to the middle of the first millennium after Christ. For many centuries important Buddhist centers were also found along the eastern coast of India, and scholars and students from all these Buddhist centers regularly visited each other and exchanged texts and doctrines. Gradually, the older Hindu beliefs reasserted themselves in India, but both to the south in Ceylon and to the east in Southeast Asia, Theravada Buddhism became the most important religious creed. In Ceylon, Buddhism became the national religion and it was to Ceylon that the Burmese and Thai eventually came to look for the source of the purest doctrine.

Buddhism must have first reached Southeast Asia directly from India, however, and it came in mixed form. Inscriptions suggest the presence of Theravada doctrines as early as the sixth century, but there is equally early evidence for the presence of other schools as well. Upper Burma seems to have had contact with both China and Tibet, which were then acquiring forms of Buddhism rather distinct from that which finally became dominant in Southeast Asia. At first the people of Burma probably sampled all the schools.

Burmese tradition holds that Buddhism came to their forefathers during the time of the great King Anawrata, who reigned from 1044 to 1077 at Pagan. Pagan is always spoken of as the first capital of the Burmese and its founding is said to go back to 849, but it was King Anawrata who first united Burma politically and who laid the basis for the subsequent glory of his capital. Even more than for his political accomplishments, he is remembered for having brought Theravada Buddhism to his people. According to tradition, he was greatly influenced by a monk from Thaton in the Mon kingdom (in southern Burma). This monk, Thera Arahanta, persuaded the king to break up the heretical religious communities which still flourished and to propagate the only true religion. The king then asked the Mons for relics of the Buddha and for a copy of the sacred Buddhist literature, but his requests were contemptuously declined. Being a man of action, Anawrata dispatched an army, conquered the Mons and carried off to his capital at Pagan not only the scriptures and relics he had requested, but all the monks and nobles of the defeated capital as well. Anawrata now looked to these captured Mon authorities—and, beyond them, to Ceylon—for guidance in the true faith.

This picture of Burmese conquest and subsequent conversion to the true Buddhist faith is a vital element in Burmese tradition, but as historical fact it is surely oversimplified. The people of the Pyu kingdom which flourished between the sixth and ninth centuries, just before the rise of Pagan, were already Buddhists—although, like the later Burmese, they had a mixture of other beliefs as well. The Pyu are always spoken of as a distinct and rather mysterious "race" that disappeared after their capital was plundered in 832. After this time the Burmese are supposed to have overrun the country after invading from the north, and become dominant. However, there is no real evidence for massive Burmese migrations, and all we really know is that one capital, that of the Pyu, declined and another, Pagan, arose. The languages used in the inscriptions of the two capitals were different, but they were certainly related, and to judge by the few available shreds of evidence, the Pyu language may even have been rather closely related to later Burmese. One cannot even rule out the possibility that Burmese was originally a dialect closely related to Pyu, a dialect that could have long been established in the plains. Certainly the Burmese of Pagan shared much with their predecessors. Theravada Buddhism had existed in Burma long before Anawrata was king, and other forms of Buddhism and other religious beliefs survived long after his death. Even this supposedly orthodox king included shrines to the thirty-seven *nats* (as the Burmese call their spirits) within the most important pagoda built under his rule.

Anawrata was not the first Buddhist king in Burma, and he was not the first to rule a country whose population was Tibeto-Burman in speech. Yet Anawrata has come to symbolize to the Burmese the founding of their nation, and it is not unfair to look upon him as a symbol of the fusion of the influences from India with the traits long native to Southeast Asia. In the end it matters little whether or not the Burmese can be said to have invaded from the north. Perhaps their language, certainly one of the important items of the cultural synthesis that was to become Burma, did indeed come from the north in the centuries preceding Anawrata's reign, but many other equally important elements in that synthesis came from the south and west, and the largest portion of the population's genetic composition probably came directly from the people who had been living there for centuries. Agricultural methods and probably family customs and the practice of spirit worship were derived without break from the Pyu and from the Mons in the south. The Mons were never quite so different from the Burmese as tradition has made them seem, and the two groups came to merge more and more. These genetic, religious, cultural, and linguistic elements fused together at Pagan, and the synthesis became the basis of the Burmese civilization that persists today.

After the time of Anawrata, the Buddhist centers on the coast of eastern India declined, and the Burmese came to regard Ceylon as the center of the purest Theravada Buddhism. About 1200, a century after Anawrata's death, a group of monks came to Burma from Ceylon claiming to represent the only orthodox Singhalese monastic order and to be uniquely empowered to give further ordination in

Burma. They refused to recognize the orthodoxy of other monks, and a distinction arose between the old Burmese and the newer Singhalese schools. Over the next centuries, the newer sect triumphed not only in upper Burma but in the Mon country as well, and Singhalese Buddhism became accepted in all of Burma as the most orthodox school.

Pagan remained the capital of most of lowland Burma for two hundred years after Anawrata's death, but in 1287 after declining in strength for several decades and arrogantly defying the Mongols who had become the masters of China, Pagan fell to Mongol conquest and its greatness came to an end.

Burma then passed through a period of anarchy. In the south, the Mons reasserted their independence and in the north Shans came down from the mountains, bringing turmoil to the countryside as they carved out chieftaincies for themselves. The Burmese did not again become political masters of most of the country until the sixteenth century, and even after that time there was almost unceasing rivalry with the Mons in the south and the Shans in the east, but time was on the side of the Burmese. Shan power was eventually confined to the hills, while the Mons were reduced to a small and politically helpless minority. The Burmese emerged with a memory of the great days of Pagan and with much of their culture still reflecting that period.

The legacy of Pagan and of the elements that merged there is nowhere more evident today than in Burmese religious life. Ever since the time of Pagan, the Burmese have been building pagodas. Some, like the famous Shwe Dagon in Rangoon, rise several hundred feet in the air and are covered by layer upon layer of gold leaf. Others are no taller than a man and except when new and whitewashed, they may be little more than a pile of crumbling masonry. Pagodas are found in the cities, in the villages, and in the fields and forests. On the hills around Mandalay they bristle from every ridge and peak. Whatever their size, Burmese pagodas are built of solid masonry with no interior spaces. Buddhists have always built stupas to mark relics of the Buddha, and pagodas are the Burmese equivalent of stupas. Indeed, the Burmese have been the most enthusiastic stupa builders of all Buddhists. Their pagodas are usually shaped rather like a bell, with a large base and a tapering spire that is surmounted by a metal "umbrella" often covered with gold leaf and always hung with bells.

Every faithful Burmese Buddhist tries to build up his stock of merit, for the merit accumulated in this life determines one's station in the next existence and nudges one along the road to Nirvana. One of the most frequent ways to acquire merit is to give food to the monks, but any religious act—donating a bell to a monastery, helping to finance the initiation of a boy into the monkhood, building a pagoda—helps. By following all the injunctions of Buddhism, and by leading the moral life that this implies, a man should gradually store up his supply of merit. Yet there is little urgency in this, for merit not accumulated in this existence may be acquired in the next. Far from grimly striving to reach Nirvana rapidly, the Burmese Buddhist knows that he has many, many lifetimes ahead of him. By the same token, breaking the precepts of Buddhism leads inevitably to demerits, but these can be canceled out by meritorious deeds. The Buddha enjoined his followers to refrain from taking life, and Burmese usually brush insects off rather than slap them. But few Burmese are vegetarians; if somebody else kills an animal, one loses no merit by eating it. Fishermen avoid the sin of taking life by not killing the fish at all, though it is surely convenient that fish die when they come out of water. A man's spiritual state is his own responsibility, and he is answerable to no priest and to no anthropomorphic deity for his behavior. So long as a man tries his best, he need not feel anxiety over his failures, but the quest for merit pervades his life.

The Burmese and their neighbors in Southeast Asia have been criticized by stern Westerners for lacking the kind of driving ambition which could build up a business and accumulate capital and which seems essential to economic development in the modern world. But it is only fair to credit them with more noble goals. The accumulation of merit builds up an even more important kind of capital: unlike material wealth, it can be taken to the next existence.

An important means of spiritual advancement is the monkhood. Buddhist orders can be entered and left at will, and although some men remain in the monkhood for life, others join for only a few weeks or months. A man may join and leave more than once. Most boys join at least briefly and the first initiation is one of the most important events in a boy's life. It usually takes place when he is twelve or fourteen years old, although boys as young as six or seven sometimes temporarily put on the yellow robe. The first initiation re-enacts the moment in the life of the Buddha when he renounced his worldly riches and went forth as a humble mendicant. During the ceremony, each boy is dressed in elegant jewelry and robes of bright colored silk and paraded around the village, traditionally on horseback, occasionally on elephants, and—in modern times—sometimes in jeeps. Feasting, music, dancing, and public entertainment engulf the community so that the initiation becomes a public festival witnessed and enjoyed by everyone. These luxuries and festivities symbolize the worldly pursuits the boys are renouncing. The boys' heads are shaved, they are ceremonially given a new name and are invested with the simple yellow robes which replace their princely attire.

The boys first become novices, the lowest rank of the holy orders, but—like the senior monks—they observe certain strict rules. The monkhood is celibate, but according to those who have endured the rules, the more difficult restriction is that which prohibits the eating of any warm food after midday. Predictably, novices and monks eat a large meal just before noon as well as one earlier in the morning. The life of the monks is supposed to be simple but not ascetic. They eat the food that is placed in their begging bowls and have only a minimum of personal possessions. Their robes are the simplest of garments, and their heads are shaved so that they need not be bothered with the care of their hair or be tempted to vanity. Monks are supposed to meditate on the principle that their attire is designed only to shield the body and not to decorate it, but in a sense this effort to renounce worldly beauty has failed, for one of Burma's most beautiful sights is that of the yellow-robed monks gracefully making their rounds.

Although Buddhist monks should be free from mundane cares and should be allowed to spend their time in meditation and religious pursuits, they have not been such a total drain on the resources of their communities as some Westerners have charged. They have presided at monastic schools which teach children the rudiments of reading and writing and provide some instruction in

the sacred literature. This instruction has been responsible for giving the Theravada Buddhist countries some of the highest literacy
rates in Asia. In recent decades, the monastic schools have had
competition from secular schools which offer a more practical route
to government service and to the higher education that has become
increasingly popular, but monastic schools still thrive.

Monks set an example of piety for all to follow, but their quest is
a personal one and they do not minister to an organized congrega-
tion. Laymen do not restrict their support to a single monk or their
attendance to a single monastery. Monks are organized under the
leadership of a head monk or abbot, and monasteries are, in turn,
organized into districts and ultimately into nationwide bodies
which exercise some degree of authority over the order. In principle
a monk can be expelled for breaking his vows, but the nature of
Buddhist belief leaves the actions of the monk largely a matter for
self-discipline, and formal discipline is rare. The devotions of the
layman are private too. He can repeat the sacred formulae in his
home or visit a pagoda by himself, and yet the support of the
monks and their monasteries and the organization of festivals, requires the cooperation of the community.

Inevitably, the laity are less concerned in their daily life with
religious matters than are the monks, but every Burmese home has a
Buddha shelf. This is a place of honor on which are kept sacred
objects, almost always including a statue of the Buddha. The shelf
is periodically adorned with flowers, and before it family members
recite chants which honor the Buddha and help them to concentrate on the great truths the Buddha taught. On duty days the
people visit a pagoda, each going to the place in the pagoda that is
set aside for those born on a particular day of the week. They bow,
offer some flowers, pour a libation, chant, meditate on the truths of
the religion, and perhaps gain realization that the world is one of
suffering and that the only escape is to reduce one's wants. After-
ward, they may retire with their families and friends to a corner of
the pagoda to smoke large Burmese cheroots, and perhaps to eat a
picnic lunch or pass a pleasant hour chatting and joking. The Westerner who expects only solemnity in a religious structure is likely to
be surprised by such conviviality, but Burmese Buddhism is less
solemn in practice than in theory, and repose, encouraged by the

peaceful statues of the Buddha and the gentle tinkling of bells, is more characteristic of Burmese religious gatherings than solemnity.

Nat *Worship*

Buddhism deals with remote ends, but does little to shield men from the crises of everyday life. It provides no cures for disease, no concrete formulae to deal with misfortune, no solace for the terrified. With no gods to pray to, Burmese Buddhists turn instead to astrology, charms, omens, and—above all—to the propitiation of the *nats*. Like the spirits worshipped by most hill peoples, Burmese *nats* are everywhere—in the house, in the air, in the water, and in the forest—and they are blamed for most of life's misfortunes. To keep the *nats* at bay, the Burmese hold a vast variety of rituals, based upon less systematic theology than are the Buddhist rituals, but no less demanding of time and energy. Burmese recognize thirty-seven chief *nats* and a host of lesser ones. To placate them, the people erect shrines near their houses and outside their villages. These shrines are often shaped like little boxes and have an image of a *nat* within, before which the people leave offerings of food and flowers.

To a woman who knows how to ask them, *nats* will give information about the future. The woman works herself into such a trance that the *nat* can possess her and speak through her. Onlookers may then address questions to the *nat* and their answers will come back in a strange and distorted voice, showing that it is not the medium who speaks but the *nat*. Even the great annual festivals of the Burmese—the Water Festival in the spring, when people sprinkle one another with water as a gesture of honor, and the Festival of Lights in the fall, when candles shine from the windows of every home—are fundamentally in honor of the *nats* although, like the pagan elements of Christmas, they have been incorporated into the practices of the other religion.

Travelers put flowers or food in altars by the side of the road. Truckdrivers try to assure themselves a safe journey by tying flowers to their radiator caps as offerings to the *nat*. An epidemic may be attributed to a *nat* and can be dealt with by noisy ceremonies intended to frighten it away. The household *nat* must be appeased with offerings, lest he bring harm to the family, but he may help guard the house against outsiders if he can be persuaded to confine his malice to strangers.

Buddhism and *nat* worship have long coexisted and have become intricately intertwined, but they have never fully merged. As modern medicine and other new methods of dealing with man's ancient problems of disease and hunger spread among the Burmese, it is possible that those elements of their ritual life directed toward the *nat* will become less popular. Science may be more successful in coping with these problems. But Buddhism, with its attention upon far more eternal questions, is less susceptible to such displacement. A century of foreign rule did nothing to weaken Buddhism. Indeed the religion became something of a nationalist symbol to the Burmese—a rallying point for their resistance to British rule. U Nu, the first prime minister of independent Burma, was a deeply religious man and although, like King Anawrata nine hundred years ago, he participated not only in the strictly Buddhist ceremonies but regularly presided over offerings to the *nats* as well, he regarded his support and encouragement of Buddhism as among his most important programs. There seems little prospect for any serious secularization of Burmese belief or practice.

Chapter Seven

The Thai

Origin and Spread of the Thai

Today, the central part of the Southeast Asian mainland is dominated by speakers of Thai: the Thai themselves, the Laotians, and the Shans of parts of Burma and Yunnan. Their languages, are almost mutually intelligible but are quite different from those of other Southeast Asians, and this seems to set them off as a special set of peoples. If their languages had not spread fairly recently from some common center, they would be more diversified than they are, and considerable speculation has been directed toward guessing the location of this point of origin of the Thai language.

Until the thirteenth century, a kingdom known to the Chinese as Nanchao flourished in what is now Yunnan. Students of Southeast Asian history have traditionally referred to Nanchao as a Thai kingdom and have suggested that it was from here that the Thai language and people subsequently spread. Unfortunately, the evidence for this hypothesis is meager, and it has been perpetuated largely by scholars echoing the theories of their predecessors. The sole direct evidence of the language of Nanchao seems to be a short list of words recorded in Chinese characters. At best, the characters give only a rough indication of the pronunciation, but even with the most tolerant judgment it is hard to see more than a handful of Thai-like words, and similarities to Tibeto-Burman (conceivably Lolo, a group of Tibeto-Burman languages still widely spoken in Yunnan) are just as easy to find.

If one ignores the flimsy evidence of this list and considers only the present distribution of the Thai languages, a rather different location emerges as their most likely point of origin. Several other languages fall into the same family as Thai, Shan, and Laotian though they are not quite so closely related as these are to each other. The more remote relatives are all spoken in northern Vietnam and in the adjacent regions of southern China, well to the east of what was once the Nanchao kingdom. It is tempting to look upon this area of greatest linguistic diversity as the center from which the Thai languages spread, and nothing in the known history of the Thai would contradict such a guess. Certainly the early speakers of Thai must have been strongly influenced by the Chinese, for the language is still replete with words borrowed from Chinese, but this could have happened as easily along the China-Vietnam border as in Yunnan.

Speakers of Thai can first be identified with some confidence in the early twelfth century, when they formed a number of small states or chieftaincies in the upper valley of the Menam around the fringes of northern Thailand, and it has been claimed that some of the soldiers depicted on the bas-reliefs at Angkor represent Thai mercenaries. By the next century Thai-speaking chieftaincies had spread more widely: 1229 is the traditional date for the establishment of the Ahom kingdom all the way west in Assam, where a Thai-speaking aristocracy ruled for several centuries (the name *Assam* is derived from *Ahom,* and ultimately comes from the same source as both *Shan* and *Siam*). Other Thai-speaking states were established in upper Burma at about the same time, and still other Thai were then fighting with the Cambodians of Angkor.

It was, however, not until after the Mongol conquest that the greatest Thai expansion occurred. From their bases in China, the Mongols conquered Nanchao in 1253 and overthrew Pagan in 1287. In the succeeding centuries Thai appear to be everywhere. Thai speakers established themselves as the governing population, through the Burmese Shan states and in much of Yunnan, and their rule spread southward out of the mountains onto the plains of Thailand and eastward onto the plains of Burma and Assam. It was to be a hundred years before the Thai conquerors in upper Burma became assimilated into the general Burmese culture and it was even longer before the Ahom dynasty in Assam finally ended, though by that time the culture of the conquerors had been much modified by their subjects. In Thailand, the language of the conquerors took hold and both the Mon and the Khmer languages, which had been spoken there before, steadily retreated.

It is difficult to account in an entirely satisfactory manner for this rapid spread of Thai rule. It is too simple to say that the Thai exploded outward from Nanchao after its defeat by the Chinese, and yet some powerful forces apparently gave them an advantage over the older kingdoms they defeated. In part, the Thai may have been deliberately encouraged by the Mongols, who could count upon them to bring disunity to China's southern borders and thereby to facilitate the defense of China. To the people of the ancient Southeast Asian kingdoms, the Thai must have seemed like barbarians and perhaps, like other barbarians, they had a fearlessness in battle that served them well in their wars with older, more settled peoples. If so, they were sophisticated barbarians, for their northern origins had certainly put them into close contact with the Chinese, from whom they must have learned something of the arts of war and government which possibly gave them a decisive advantage over their opponents.

Of course, the Thai conquests did not necessarily involve mass displacement of the population. In northern Burma and in Assam, the languages of the conquered populations eventually reasserted themselves, and although Shan came to be the dominant language in the mountain valleys of Laos, the Burmese Shan States, much of Yunnan, and among the chiefs who ruled from these valleys, the various tribal languages are still spoken in the higher mountains. Shan became the language of the upper class; and any man, whatever his ancestry, is likely to adopt the Shan language if he can practice wet rice farming and especially if he has serious political aspirations. Only in Thailand and in lowland Laos did Thai become the language of the entire population.

It is reasonable to guess that the political forms which the Shan states of Burma retained until very recently were much like those of the earliest Thai chieftaincies. Only the dominant and ruling Shans give any unity to the ethnic jumble of the Shan states. The mountains are intersected by river valleys and, where the land is low and flat enough to permit wet rice to be grown, Shan farmers and a Shan chief or "Sawbwa" are usually found. Each valley usually forms the center of a little domain over which a Sawbwa ruled. In the hills all around are tribesmen who follow their own customs, speak their own language, and owed only a minimum of allegiance to the Sawbwa.

Though their numbers have never been large, the valley people organize their agriculture, their families, and their religious life much as do the Burmese or the lowland Thai. The courts of the Sawbwas reflected, in miniature, the pomp of the royal courts. The title of *Sawbwa*, like that of *king*, passed from father to son, and so far as possible the ritual of the court imitated the elegant ritual of the Burmese palace. The Sawbwas, however, were only partially independent. They relied upon the people within their domains for support, but their territories were too small to achieve real safety from attack. Sawbwas contended for power among themselves, and into these troubled waters the more powerful lowland rulers could sometimes fish with profit. As a result, each Sawbwa offered a loose allegiance to one of his more powerful neighbors. The threat of Burmese, Thai, or Chinese intervention may have brought an occasional degree of stability to the states, but the mountainous terrain made it impossible for the plains powers to assert full control over their vassals. The Sawbwas, in brief, had a position not unlike the lords of feudal Europe: they depended upon the support of their subjects, owed a limited allegiance to a more powerful king, and continually competed with one another.

If the first Thai chieftaincies were organized in this feudal manner, then those Thai who moved southward into the plains would have had to modify their political ideas before they could hope to create a united country. They changed, in part, by copying the governmental forms they found in the plains, but they also developed administrative techniques new to Southeast Asia.

Their first capital in southern Thailand was Ayuthia, founded in 1350. At first the kingdom seems to have been organized along feudal lines, the rulers of the provinces acting with considerable independence of the capital. By the fifteenth century, however, a shift toward a more centralized government was under way. The national administration was divided into ministries—the royal household, finance, local government, agriculture—a functional division that surpassed governmental forms in either Burma or Cambodia and may well have been based upon Chinese models. Provincial officials came increasingly to gain their office by appointment from the central government, rather than by inheritance. They were made subject to dismissal and, as a result, became more responsive to central authority. Even as late as the nineteenth century, however, the Thai government maintained a loose feudal suzerainty over some of the more distant states of Laos. The Shan Sawbwas offered their allegiance to the more distant and therefore less threatening Burmese king, and by this means kept their independence of neighboring Thailand.

For their court rituals, the Thai borrowed from their neighbors. Shivaite rites, much like those of Cambodia, still validate the authority of the Thai king, and other religious and philosophical ideas came from Burma, where Theravada Buddhism had become dominant by the time of the Thai conquest. Later the Thai, like the Burmese, dealt directly with Ceylon, but their first mentors of the Theravada doctrine were their closer neighbors. The Thai language had conquered the Menam basin, but in religion and in many aspects of political organization, the culture of the Menam had overcome the conquerors.

Thai Village Life

In spite of the conquest and the shift in language, the life of the villagers cannot have been radically changed. In fact, the villages of Thailand, Burma, Laos, and Cambodia are similar in so many ways that a description of one country can often stand as well for the others. Most of what has been said about Burmese Buddhism is true of Buddhism in Thailand and Cambodia, and for other aspects of life the Thai village can be taken as reasonably representative.

River valleys form the heart of each country: the Chao Praya and its tributaries which form the Menam Basin in Thailand, the Irrawady and Salween in Burma, the Mekong in both Cambodia and Laos. Large alluvial plains surround each river, and together with those in adjoining South Vietnam they produce the world's greatest amount of surplus rice. The rivers have been the people's highways and the Thai, like their neighbors, have traditionally strung their villages out along the banks of rivers or canals instead of knotting them together in clusters. Today, as roads become increasingly important, some villages line roads instead. The fields stretch out behind the houses, away from the river or road. The villages are rarely built so closely together that no open country lies between them; the physical and social boundaries dividing neighboring villages are generally clear. Each village may have from fifty to two hundred households, and as many as five hundred people. The houses are substantial, rectangular, gabled buildings and are usually built on stilts several feet above the ground as a protection against floods, animals, and thieves. Some houses are built with posts and planks of teak and corrugated iron roofs, but most are of bamboo with thatched roofs.

The work of the village revolves around the production of wet rice by the technique widely used in Asia. In much of lower Thailand and Burma, rice has been almost the only crop grown, but in other parts of these countries more reliance has been placed upon secondary crops, and in Thailand since 1955 such crops as maize, jute, and peanuts have rather suddenly become important exports. In spite of a few experiments with mechanization, rice agriculture remains almost entirely dependent upon hand labor. Even in Thailand, where mechanization has had more chance than in any neighboring country, the most a farmer has been able to hope for is a gasoline pump to assist in irrigation. The heaviest work is the transplanting and the harvest, and even schoolchildren are given vacations to help their families to finish in time. Cooperative work groups are often organized for the heaviest jobs. The owner of the padi provides his helpers with cheroots to smoke and betel mixture to chew, but he is likely to pay them not with money but by working on their fields on another day. When they work in large groups the job is lightened. Young people joke, tease, toss mud at each other, and race to see who can work fastest. Boys and girls work together and labor parties provide an opportunity for flirtation. Boys may hire themselves out at transplanting, almost as much to meet girls as to earn their pay.

Thai farmers keep a few domestic animals. Buffalos are needed for plowing and harrowing the fields before they are planted, and a farmer who does not own a buffalo must rent one. Chickens and, more rarely, pigs may be raised, but Buddhist prohibitions against killing discourage intensive animal husbandry. Instead of butchering their pigs, farmers are more likely to sell them live to Chinese merchants. Fish is the most important source of protein, and is eaten in some form at almost every meal. Farmers regularly buy dried fish, and the rivers, canals, irrigation ditches, and even rice fields yield fresh fish, crabs, and shrimp. Nets, lines, or traps are used to catch them, and they are eaten fresh or preserved by salting or fermenting. A few villagers practice such crafts as carpentry or hat-weaving, but the work of Chinese artisans and the spread of manufactured goods have undercut many of the older Thai crafts. Most villagers in Thailand are, above all, rice farmers.

Like the Burmese and Cambodians, but unlike either the Chinese or Indians the Thai do not idealize large, extended families. Many Thai families are no larger than a typical American family, though it is not unusual for one of the youngest children—in some parts of Thailand, it is most likely to be the youngest daughter; in others, the youngest son—to stay home after marriage. The young couple care for the parents and usually inherit the house and its compound. Older daughters often live at home for a while after marriage, but when the first child is born they are expected to set up independent households with their husbands. Whether the couple choose to live near the husband's family or the wife's family often depends upon their prospects for inheritance, for girls share with their brothers in the inheritance of rice lands—a striking example of the importance of the female side of the family. The father does not have the same pervading authority that a Chinese father traditionally wields, and his children have no exaggerated duty or obligation to him. Women are free to assert themselves in family affairs and even in the village decisions. Women do most of the buying and selling at the markets, and they usually handle the daily finances of the household. The poise and quiet self-confidence with which these women handle themselves in business and on public occasions always strikes the observant visitor as a distinguishing mark of Southeast Asian nations.

Yet Theravada Buddhism assigns to men an unambiguous ritual superiority. Though religious orders exist for women, they are smaller and carry much less prestige than those for men. The Thai wife shows formal respect to her husband in many symbolic ways. Like the talented servant who honors, cherishes, and cares for his slightly feckless master, the Thai wife must never suggest by word

or deed her own superiority. In 1916, all Thai were directed by
royal decree to choose family names which children would take
from their fathers, but even today these names are little used except
on formal documents. (The Burmese still resist even this suggestion
of paternal dominance and use no family names at all. A Burmese
woman does not take her husband's name, and the children's
names bear no necessary resemblance to those of either of their
parents.) By minimizing the importance of the family name, the
Thai give even less recognition than Europeans to the kinship bond
which could tie related families together. In their customs of equal
inheritance, the ease with which women participate in family decisions, and the equal importance of kinsmen related through the
maternal or paternal line, these families are far more similar to
those of the modern West than to those of India or China.

Kinship ties beyond one's immediate family are, however, by no
means ignored by the Thai or by other lowland Southeast Asians,
and in certain respects they are probably more important than in
the West. For example, marriages in rural Thailand often take
place between members of the same village, and so over the course
of a few generations almost everyone in a village comes to be related to everyone else, and the village itself can be looked upon as a
loose kinship group. Of course some fellow villagers are more
closely related than others, and the complexity of interweaving relationships allows people to emphasize these bonds when it is convenient and minimize or ignore them when it is not. One can exchange
labor or borrow money or property more readily from a kinsman,
for kinsmen are expected to be generous and kind to one another.
Therefore a man who wants help from another will call upon kinship to justify his request, while he will ignore another kinsman
with whom he has no dealings. If a man moves to a new village, any
kinsmen who already live there—even distant cousins—may make
the move relatively easy. Any wealthy man is expected to help out
his more needy relatives, and this may have helped to prevent the
concentration of wealth in the hands of a few people. On the other
hand, this obligation may also have made it difficult for Southeast
Asians to mobilize entrepreneurial skills, for any successful businessman is in danger of having his rewards drained away when his

less affluent relatives begin to emphasize the importance of their kinship ties.

Thai babies are constantly carried, cuddled, and fondled, and they are nursed whenever they show signs of hunger. The anthropologist Ruth Benedict suggested that Thai parents tend to leave the steps in maturation to nature and to the responsibility of the child himself. With quiet coaching, but with no sense of urgency, babies learn to walk. They wear nothing but a shirt, and nobody becomes upset when the baby soils the floor or someone's lap, for adults know that eventually the growing child himself will learn self-control. Nevertheless, children are expected to develop a kind of self-reliance that can be seen as anticipating the behavior of adults. Thai are often described as self-reliant; even their Buddhist religion emphasizes the personal quest for enlightenment and leaves its pursuit to the individual's own initiative. Nevertheless, older children can be vigorously punished when naughty, and although verbal threats are usually sufficient, they are spanked if necessary. Children may also be threatened with animals or spirits and in this way frightened into obedience.

Whether through indulgence or strict discipline—or, more likely, through a subtle combination of the two—Thai children do learn to be courteous and respectful at a remarkably early age. A child soon learns the differences in status among the people around him. His parents will press his palms together and hold them to his forehead to show respect for the monks, and he soon learns to raise them to his face for his parents. Just as men are ritually superior to women, so older people are superior to younger, and a child must learn the ceremonious respect due his elders. Later he will also learn to grant the formal respect due to government officials and, above them, to royalty. Thai do not expect to associate with others as equals; everyone is seen as either superior or inferior. One cannot even speak the Thai language without indicating something about one's status, for pronouns vary with the rank of the speaker and that of the person to whom he speaks. To some extent status is determined by birth, but because one's status at birth is attributed to the accumulation of merit in former existences, it has, in a sense, been earned. All men can look forward to the increase in status brought by age and all men can join the monkhood and acquire the highest formal status of all. All such status differences seem well deserved and are accepted as part of the natural order. No one need resent his own position, and he need not fawn on his superiors or be arrogant to his subordinates, for they do not threaten it. Moreover, all the symbols of status, from the deference with which a woman treats her husband to the prostration once required of subjects in the presence of the king, are merely formalities which help to keep life orderly; they carry no implication of degradation. Even a child is assured his own place of dignity.

As children grow up, they play games which imitate the activities of their elders. They plow imaginary fields and cook imaginary food. By the age of seven or eight, a girl may be put in charge of a small brother or sister, and she soon starts to help with the household chores. A boy's first job is often to tend his father's water buffalo. Since he joins his friends who are watching their own buffalo, it is a sociable task.

By Asian standards, Thai are relatively free to choose their spouses, although young people are expected to seek the advice and approval of their parents. The veranda of the girl's home is the traditional courting place, and here in the evening the boy may come to recite poems to her and exchange pleasant chatter. But the parents are never far away, and the boy should not so much as touch a girl before their marriage. It has been claimed that since the most honored way of life open to a man, the monkhood, is dedicated to celibacy, Thai men do not have to "prove" their manhood by sexual adventures.

Once a couple obtain the approval of their parents, the marriage itself is a simple matter. If the families are wealthy, gifts may be exchanged and a property settlement agreed upon to establish the new couple satisfactorily. Sometimes a small bride price is paid, but usually the bride and groom simply begin living together and are then accepted as married. Elopement is recognized as an alternative for headstrong couples who cannot obtain their parents' permission. A couple who elope may eventually be forgiven, and the new son-in-law often comes to be accepted by his wife's parents. Buddhism has nothing to say about marriage, and no Buddhist ceremonies take place at the wedding. The celibate monks cannot be expected to give sanction to such a worldly relationship. Divorce is possible by the mutual consent, but it is rare after children have been born.

Thai villages have traditionally been quite autonomous. Each has a headman, now elected by adult franchise from among the respected and well-to-do farmers. The election must be approved by some higher agency of government, but such approval is usually routine. Once chosen, the headman usually retains his position until death or retirement. He must be among the wealthier members of the village, for he must offer a certain amount of hospitality to visitors and he is expected to contribute generously to the temple. He receives informal advice from other older and respected villagers, and together this group of men usually can guide the village. The headman forms a crucial link between the villagers and the district headquarters, which may supervise many hundreds of villages and is the local arm of the central government. He keeps track of births and deaths and passes on these vital statistics to the district offices. Traditionally, he has also been responsible for the maintenance of law and order within his village, and although the central government now takes an increasing part in the arrest and punishment of criminals, local disputes among villagers are still often arbitrated by the headman. The headman directs labor parties that work to maintain local roads and canals. He also attends monthly meetings held by the district officer, at which he receives information about public health, schools, elections, or irrigation problems, and he passes the government's directives down to the villagers.

In the past, the villages of Southeast Asia could expect little from the central governments. At most, they might have protection from bandits or insurrection. A few village youths have always been drawn into military service. Thailand has conscription today, and although only a small proportion of boys are called into the army, military service is an important channel by which knowledge of the modern world seeps into the villages. Many boys never leave their native region except during their army career. Today, of course, all the central governments take an increasingly active interest in local affairs and attempt to provide a variety of services which were formerly ignored or left entirely to the villagers. Medical assistants vaccinate the children, spray DDT about the villages, and make medical suggestions. More and more villages acquire schoolteachers; some efforts are made to encourage new agricultural techniques; everywhere there are policemen and tax collectors.

Like the Burmese, the Thai combine a concern for the spirits with their devotion to Buddhism. Sickness is generally attributed to malevolent spirits. Thai hang food from a post in the corner of their fields before plowing as an offering to the spirit of the land. Bits of food, flowers, tobacco, and the betel mixture are offered to the rice goddess when the seedbed is prepared.

At one side of every prosperous Thai village is a religious center or *wat* with a temple, a dormitory for monks and novices, and sometimes a stupa and a special school building. The temple roofs are usually built in tiers and glazed with colorful tiles, forming one of the loveliest features of the Thai countryside. Like the stupas characteristic of Burma, the Thai temples show a devotion to values higher than worldly materialism, yet at the same time they please one's sense of beauty. The religious festivals serve to emphasize the great truths of Buddha's teachings, but they are also a time for friendly gatherings and for the enjoyment of drum and gong music, dramas and puppet shows, and the angular dancing in which everyone delights. This balance between worldly satisfactions and devotion to nonworldly goals seems to be built into every Thai. As the Thai pursue their goals, they show a buoyancy and spontaneity which should well be the envy of all. Concerned with ultimate destiny but accepting of this world's condition, Southeast Asians seem to have achieved a humility without servility and a pride without arrogance.

Chapter Eight

The Vietnamese

○

The Chinese Influence

Although Southeast Asia owes less of its civilization to China than to India, Chinese influence has never been lacking, and in a few areas it has been predominant. The Chinese influence was exerted in quite different manner from the Indian. So far as is known, no Indian state ever sent an army of conquest to Southeast Asia or even seriously interfered in its internal affairs, but whenever China has been unified and strong enough, she has meddled in Southeast Asian politics and from time to time has sent armies southward to enforce her edicts or to extend her territory. China may even have helped to foster disunity among the Southeast Asian people, for in the past as much as today it has been to China's advantage to keep them divided and weak.

Chinese civilization had its origins in the north, and one may look upon its spread into southern China as part of the same movement which has carried it further into Southeast Asia, as well. Most of southern China has now been thoroughly absorbed into the mainstream of Chinese civilization, but at one time its culture may not have been so very different from that of Southeast Asia. Even today many enclaves of tribal people remain in southern China, particularly in the more remote and mountainous regions. These tribes show varying degrees of Sinicization, but broadly speaking, as one goes further south the resemblances to the Chinese grow weaker.

Of the people who live south of the modern political border of China, none has been more profoundly affected by Chinese civilization than the Vietnamese, originally the inhabitants of the flat country around the Red River, in what is now North Vietnam. From here, communication with southern China is relatively easy, while the Annamite mountain chain which parallels the coast has made communication with the rest of Southeast Asia more difficult. Communication with southern China has been so easy, in fact, that northern Vietnam was incorporated into the Chinese empire as early as the second century B.C., and for a thousand years it remained an integral part of China. In 939, during the decline of the T'ang dynasty, Vietnam freed herself from Chinese rule, but the millennium of Chinese control left an indelible mark on the culture of the Vietnamese. Even their name reflects the importance of China, for *Vietnam* literally means *the southern country*, and, of course, it is only in relation to China that it can be considered "southern." Perhaps the surprising thing is that the Vietnamese still have anything at all left of their Southeast Asian heritage.

Even after regaining their independence, the Vietnamese looked north to China as the source of wisdom and knowledge and they suffered occasional Chinese attacks. Pressed from the north by the Chinese, the Vietnamese have looked in the opposite direction, to the south, for expansion. As a result, the Vietnamese with their language and their Sinicized culture have, over the centuries, percolated down to the Mekong delta where they enveloped the older Cham population and came into contact with the Cambodians. The south has always seemed to be something of a wild frontier to the Vietnamese and has long been much less densely populated than the north.

As in the other parts of Southeast Asia, the political boundaries of the modern nation now encompass not only the lowlands but the bordering hills as well; but no Southeast Asian people has shunned the hills more obstinately than the Vietnamese. Their agriculture is not suitable to the hills and they have been terrified of the fever and dysentery found there. They have also believed that the mountains and forests were filled with malicious spirits, poised to harm the incautious man from the plains. Of course, the hills have never been empty of people, and the mountaineers did all they could to make their country dangerous for outsiders. As a result, the geographical boundary between plains and hills is paralleled closely by the cultural boundary between the Vietnamese and the hills tribes. The architecture, clothing, language, agriculture, and rituals all change abruptly as one enters the hills. Because in central Vietnam the mountains often reach the seacoast, the Vietnamese who live there are confined to lowland pockets, isolated from one another by intervening hills. Thus the Vietnamese are concentrated in the plains in the north and in the south of the country, and scattered only thinly between. This distribution has given rise to the frequent comparison of the country with two rice baskets, the north and the south, joined by a slender carrying pole. The population of the northern delta is larger and far more dense and, in fact, this is the only area of mainland Southeast Asia that has produced the dense population so characteristic of other parts of Asia.

The Government Hierarchy

Just as the people further west took over Indian political doctrines and patterned their government upon Indian conceptions, so the Vietnamese took over the ideas of China. Perhaps this imitation was most rapid during the time of Chinese rule, but even in independence Vietnam retained a governmental system which closely followed Chinese lines. The Vietnamese emperor sat at the pinnacle of civil and military power and, like his Chinese counterpart, he bore the title "Son of Heaven." None but he was permitted to make the annual offerings to heaven at the state ceremonies. Before the ceremony, he and the ministers who assisted him purified themselves for three days and then, to the ringing of bells and beating of drums, they would roast a young buffalo and ritually bury its blood and hair. On top of a rounded hillock at altars of heaven, earth, and the ancestors of the royal dynasty, he would then offer jade, silk, rice, meat, and flowers, and invoke the blessing of the spirits. This ceremony served to validate the emperor's unique status in the nation, not only as temporal ruler, but as the supreme ritual leader, and nothing symbolizes the passing of the old order so clearly as the cessation of the state ceremonies after 1942.

Confucius, whom the Vietnamese have honored as highly as have the Chinese, specified five important social relationships: the respect of the subject for his prince; that of the son for his father; that of the wife for her husband; that of the younger brother for his elder brother; and that of a friend for his friend. The subject should, in principle, follow his emperor in blind obedience and devotion, just as the son should follow his father. Yet blind obedience to an incompetent emperor could be disastrous and as in any political system, problems arose from time to time regarding the legitimacy of the emperor's rule. These made it doubtful whether the emperor had the "mandate of heaven" to rule his people. Here, Vietnam borrowed the Chinese theory that legitimacy is confirmed by the prosperity of the state. When the country was prosperous and the people healthy, then it was clear that the emperor did indeed have the mandate; when things went badly, that was a sign that the emperor had "lost" the mandate, so the people were justified in rebelling. How deeply this abstract justification of rebellion was felt by the common people is difficult to know, but in the final days of French rule the doctrine must have seemed rather tarnished to a good many Vietnamese. Bao Dai, the last emperor of Vietnam, was the son of the former emperor by a concubine of peasant birth. He was educated in France and he had become completely Western in his tastes. The French installed him on his throne, but the real power had long passed to the colonial rulers. As the country was plunged into the violence of the Japanese conquest and then the long civil war, it must have seemed clear to anyone who still cared that Bao Dai had long ago lost the mandate of heaven.

In earlier times the emperor was surrounded by the appurtenances of divinity, though he was not quite divine himself. He lived an isolated life in an area appropriately called the "Forbidden City," into which only his wife, his concubines, his servants, and the highest government officials could enter. All his subjects prostrated themselves in his presence. The emperor was allowed to have numerous wives and concubines, and inevitably the imperial family grew very large but, as elsewhere in Southeast Asia, the range of royal kinsmen was limited by the rule that the degree of nobility was reduced with each generation removed from the royal ancestor.

The emperor was assisted by an elaborate bureaucracy. This bureaucracy or mandarinate was open to those who had passed the state examinations, which in theory were open to all men. Even the poorest boy was eligible for a post in the civil service, if he could acquire enough education to pass the examinations—but of course it would be difficult for a poor boy to achieve the necessary education. His family might not be able to spare his labor in the fields, let alone pay the price of his schooling. Yet the system of open examinations did permit a degree of social mobility, and it prevented the formation of rigidly distinct classes. Like their Chinese counterparts, the examinations were based upon the philosophical and moral teachings of the Chinese classics. Scholars studied poetry, philosophy, history, and ethics, and all education had a moral flavor. To become "educated" meant to pursue reason and to lead a life of temperance, moderation, and honesty. This education had no direct bearing upon the duties of the office to which the applicant might aspire, and the practical Westerner is likely to feel that the choice of government officials was, at best, haphazard. The theory seems to have been that any man capable of the intellectual achievement of mastering the Chinese classics could, with relative ease, turn his hand to any mundane technical tasks a bureaucrat might face.

The scholar was not expected to withdraw from the world around him, but to assume leadership in his community. Because it was the channel by which men sought to enter the mandarinate, education became the means to security and prestige. A scholar could never be expected to work with his hands, so education also meant freedom from manual labor and the assurance of honor and respect.

Education required, among other things, the mastering of the Chinese characters, for so great was the prestige of their northern neighbor that the Vietnamese used only the Chinese system of writing. This reinforced the bonds between the two countries, for it meant that all of Chinese literature and learning was available to the educated Vietnamese. As early as the seventeenth century, Catholic missionaries worked out a system of Roman transcription for the Vietnamese language, known as *quoc-ngu*. Gradually, particularly after the nineteenth-century conquest by the French, *quoc-ngu* came to replace Chinese characters as the common method of writing. This undermined the value of the older type of education and, since the competitive examinations were based upon the Chinese classics, the examinations became increasingly anachronistic. Finally, in 1915, the examinations were abolished by the French, and the break with the past was complete.

As in all of traditional Asia, the government hierarchy stood above and somewhat separate from the life of the villages. Peasant farmers have neither needed nor wanted continual direction by any central government. The village had to pay its share of taxes and contribute its labor for public works, and its youths were recruited into the national army. But as long as the village was peaceful, its internal problems were its own concern and the central government was delighted to leave it alone.

Nevertheless, the emphasis upon learning which was fostered by the examination system did affect even the internal organization of the villages. Not all those who tried to pass the examination were successful, and passing no more guaranteed entrance into the bureaucracy than a college degree guarantees a job in the modern world. Those who did enter government service often served in a different part of the country, but they always retained a loyalty to their home village and the educated people of a village, whether or not they had a post in the government, could expect to assume leadership in their own village.

There was one other requirement for village leadership: ownership of land. Education and landownership often but not always went together, for it was difficult to obtain an education except through the wealth which land brought. Scholars and landowners together formed a self-appointed "council of notables," a body of respected local aristocrats. They administered village property, organized public works, collected taxes, and policed the village territory. None of these notables was paid, although they might be reimbursed by being allowed to use a share of the village-owned land; the prestige of their position was more valued than any material reward. The council of notables selected the man for the office which has been rather poorly translated as *mayor*. Unlike the headman of Thailand, he was usually a man of relatively low prestige, a delegate of the council who was expected to carry out its orders and to do the routine clerical work of maintaining tax rolls and transacting local business with the government. One of the many difficulties which the French created in their administration of Vietnamese villages was to try to give the mayor more responsibility than he had traditionally held. Having relatively low prestige in the eyes of the villagers, he could carry out his new responsibilities only with the backing of the French, and this augmented neither his own nor the administration's prestige.

The council of notables stood between the villagers below and the bureaucracy above. A member of the bureaucracy was looked upon as a representative of the emperor, and he commanded some of the same respectful obedience due the emperor himself. The mandarinate was divided into a number of sharply defined grades or ranks, each with its own prerogatives and symbols of status. At the other end of the social scale, ordinary villagers were also assigned to one of several formal and named ranks, and each had specific rights and obligations. At the top were the notables, and at the bottom were the landless peasants who paid no tax and were scarcely considered citizens. In between were several grades based upon age and wealth. Those at the top were exempt from labor tax. Men over sixty-one had a special rank and the indigent and invalids were set aside in special lower ranks. The upper ranks ruled the village and their position was symbolized through many clear distinctions of protocol. Even the village spirits were assigned formal ranks.

This ranking system contrasts curiously with that of Burma or Thailand. The Vietnamese class system was more open than that of the other countries, since the examination system provided a built-in mechanism through which mobility could in principle be achieved, even though the majority of the population was never in a position to take advantage of it. In spite of its relative openness, the levels of status in the Vietnamese system were far more precisely defined and had far more subdivisions than those in Thailand or Burma, where the only clear divisions were those of aristocrats, monks, and commoners. The monkhood was open to all, but in Burma or Thailand there was no way by which a commoner could legitimately aspire to climb into the nobility.

Vietnamese Village Life

Farmers have never lived in isolated homesteads in northern Vietnam, but have always clustered their houses together in villages, and the members of a village seem to have emphasized their common ties even more closely than in Thailand or Burma. It is said that a Vietnamese who leaves his home village can never be happy, for he dreams constantly of the time when he can return, and the attachment to the village has even been offered as one explanation for the reluctance of Vietnamese to enter the highlands. In the mountains the fields available for wet cultivation are few and scattered, and it would be impossible to collect a large enough number of people in one place to form a viable village of the sort so greatly loved.

The unity of the village is symbolized by a ceremonial center called the *dinh*. Here, often grouped together within a walled compound, are temples dedicated to important spirits, and a place for villagers to gather and debate their affairs. Traditionally, each village has had a patron deity, chosen by the villagers, and often based upon an historical or legendary person. This deity is granted a title and a certain rank by imperial edict, and is subject to promotion or deposition by imperial order. The patron deity has its own sanctuary in the *dinh* and the villagers dutifully perform rituals in its honor. Other deities, as well, have their own temples grouped together in the *dinh*. There may be a temple to the five goddesses of metal, wood, water, fire, and earth—or to the spirits of the dead people whose descendants have ceased to worship them and who, as a result, wander about and threaten the living, but each village has its own favorite deities and need not have the same temples as its neighbors.

Although the *dinh* is the ceremonial center of the village, it does not include a residence for monks, as does the Thai *wat*. In Thailand and Burma, common support of the monks of the village monastery may emphasize the unity of the villagers, but in Vietnam the common stake in village land and property is as important as common participation in the *dinh*. Villagers in all the countries cooperate to keep local roads and canals in repair, but only in Vietnam has the private land of the farmers been traditionally supplemented by land owned collectively by the village, and only the Vietnamese cooperate to the point of storing communal stocks of grain to be used by the needy in times of shortage. Communal land was periodically distributed among villagers for their temporary use, either to notables as compensation for their work or to the poor who would otherwise have no land at all. This provided an important form of insurance against total destitution and gave everyone, rich and poor, an important stake in the village. Most land was privately owned, however, and as population has grown, the plots have tended to become more and more fragmented. In a thoroughly monetary economy, land could be rented, mortgaged, and sold, and an increasing land hunger helped fire an unrest with which the French never adequately coped.

Like all Southeast Asians, most Vietnamese are rice farmers, but regional specialization goes further than elsewhere. A few villages specialize in a single craft, such as metal work, silk production, or paper manufacture, and they exchange their products for the food and craft products of other villages. The local availability of raw materials may have encouraged this pattern, but even more important has been the strong local feeling: a man would teach his fellow villagers the secrets of his trade but he would be unwilling to instruct others, and so local monopolies would be created and protected. Along the coast, some villages derive their entire livelihood from fishing, and their boats set out each day to tap the rich reserves of the South China Sea. Here, the wealthiest villagers are the owners of the fishing boats, but their local prestige and power are comparable to those of large landowners elsewhere. Other villagers man their boats as master fishermen or as ordinary members of the crew, and often a woman goes along whose duty it is to sell the catch. Trading junks sometimes follow the fishermen and buy their catch before they ever land. With such specialization, no village can be self-sufficient, and trade in rice, fish, and manufactured goods has long been an essential part of Vietnamese life.

In the agricultural villages, rice has always been the dominant crop. As in the southern deltas of Thailand and Burma, large parts of southern Vietnam grow almost nothing but rice. In the north, rice is supplemented by such secondary crops as sweet potatoes, taro, manioc, arrowroot, areca nuts, tobacco, and tea. There the land must support an average of two people per acre of cultivated land, and much of the land in the north must bear two crops per year— either two crops of rice, or one of rice and one of some alternative crop.

Family Organization

So deeply did Chinese influence penetrate into Vietnam that it has affected the form of the family. Like the Chinese, every Vietnamese bears one of a limited number of family names, conventionally known as the "hundred surnames," inherited from his father. The Vietnamese even used Chinese characters to stand for the names. One essential feature of the Chinese system never reached Vietnam: the prohibition on marriage between people of the same surname, and Chinese travelers have remarked with surprise at this Vietnamese "peculiarity." Like the Chinese, the Vietnamese have idealized the large, extended family in which a man would gather his sons and his sons' wives and children under the same roof. As in China also, the ideal has often failed to be realized, for most Vietnamese have lived in small households of parents and children.

Older patterns of Southeast Asian life, however, seem to persist in the role which women play, for in spite of centuries of formal legal codes (copied almost verbatim from the Chinese originals), women retained the right to inherit land and property and to maintain special property rights separate from those of their husbands, in a manner quite different from that of traditional China. The codes gave women no separate right to share in the inheritance of their parents' property, but in practice women have at least been able to take dowries to their husbands. The dowry never became completely merged with the husband's property, for in the case of death or divorce, the girl or her family retained rights over it. In Vietnam, women's names even appear beside those of their husbands on titles and deeds.

Traditionally, men and women are supposed to maintain a formal separation. They may not sit on the same mat or even touch each other. Yet women do heavy work in the fields and—more often than in China—they drive oxcarts, pole sampans, and even work as porters and laborers. As elsewhere in Southeast Asia, they are considered thriftier than their husbands. Vietnamese shops, unlike those of the Chinese, are run by women—indeed, a Vietnamese man would be ridiculed for doing such "woman's work." When people work together in their fields, the formal division of the sexes may be forgotten and, like the Thai, they may tease one another and even sing risqué songs, which lighten the burden of transplanting. But that is behavior for the farmers and would be considered unrefined among the educated classes.

Kinsmen retain a formal affiliation to one another that is lacking among the plains people in the countries further west. They unite in patrilineal clans whose members cooperate in honoring their common ancestors. The clan has a ritual head, the oldest male of the senior branch. He may live in the house where the ancestral shrine is kept and he is primarily responsible for maintaining it, but his brothers and cousins join him periodically in performing the rituals. At a funeral, the eldest son of the deceased serves as the chief mourner and directs the ritual. A tablet which represents the dead man and is believed to contain his spirit is added to the ancestral altar; here, along with the other deceased members of the clan, he will be periodically honored.

The importance of this ancestor worship makes childlessness a tragedy and it is particularly essential that a son be born to the eldest branch of the family, for he will have the greatest ritual responsibility. In spite of the inequality which gives ritual leadership to the eldest brother, and in spite of the Confucian ideal which assigns to him a clearly superior position, brothers share almost equally in the inheritance of the family property. The eldest brother does inherit the inalienable and indivisable plot of land which is set aside to support ancestor rituals, but he holds it only in guardianship for his kinsmen.

Old people depend upon their sons for support, so a couple with no sons may find themselves in a difficult position. If they have a daughter, they can sometimes persuade the man she marries to move in with them and act as a son. This is a far less normal situation in Vietnam than in Thailand, and only a poor boy who recognizes the value of his wife's inheritance can be expected to take on such a role. The couple can support the girl's parents and the husband can act as a son to his wife's parents—in all ways but one: he can never take over the rituals involved in ancestor worship. These must be turned over to a more distant, but patrilineal, kinsman.

The emperor's annual sacrifice to heaven, the ceremonies to the patron deity of the village, and the rites of ancestor worship symbolize, respectively, the three most important levels of traditional Vietnamese life: the nation, the village, and the family. The sacrifice to heaven and the use of ancestor tablets were almost slavishly copied from Chinese practices, but they were not the only elements of Chinese religion to influence Vietnam.

The northern or Mahayana variety of Buddhism is quite different from that found in most of Southeast Asia, but it is the one the Vietnamese practice today. Mahayana differs from Theravada Buddhism in several ways. In the first place, Mahayana Buddhism peopled the world with deities called Boddhisatvas. Originally these were men, but in the cycle of rebirths they approached the ultimate goal of nothingness and then, out of compassion for their fellow men, they stopped short of complete annihilation and postponed their loss of individuality. The Boddhisatvas became personal and comprehensible deities (unlike anything in Theravada Buddhism) toward whom a man might direct his hopes. Mahayana Buddhists can pray to a Boddhisatva and the example of assistance to others provided by the Boddhisatvas helps to inspire Mahayana priests to give service to their fellow men. Mahayana Buddhism also has an explicit heaven and hell, to which one is assigned on the basis of his actions on earth. To be sure, the Mahayana heaven and hell are only temporary resting places on the road to Nirvana, but they may be pictured and described in terms which ordinary men can understand.

Buddhism, however, is a less important element in the ritual life of Vietnam than it is in that of other Southeast Asian countries. Far fewer Vietnamese men become monks, and those who do usually remain monks for life. They officiate at ceremonies, but do not go about begging for food. The respect for scholarship inspired by the devotion to the Confucian classics and the traditional examination system has also impelled monks to become learned men so as to win and retain the respect of the people, and the standards of scholarship among monks have probably been higher in Vietnam than elsewhere in Southeast Asia. Buddhist temples are rarer in Vietnam than in the countries to the west, and Vietnamese visit a Buddhist temple as only one among many places of worship.

Along with Confucianism and Buddhism, Taoism is generally recognized to be one of the three main elements of Chinese religious life. Taoism has probably had the least effect upon the Vietnamese, but in China it has come to embrace a host of mythical and magical practices which give comfort to the common man but are little amenable to learned systematization. The Vietnamese have been willing to use Taoist techniques of divination and magic when they seemed to work, and they have added these to their own stock of ritual procedures.

Finally, like all Southeast Asians, the Vietnamese world is filled with spirits, not only those of heaven, of the village, and of dead ancestors, but simpler nature spirits which bring misfortune in the form of accidents, sterility, disease, and death. These spirits must be propitiated to ward off evil, and the usual "cure" for sickness is to present them with food. Each craft and trade has its own patron deity and associated rituals, and farmers must regularly propitiate the spirits throughout the year. The spirit offerings seem to reach back to a far older element of Vietnamese life and indicate that Chinese influence, however profound it may have been, has not yet succeeded in obliterating the underlying Southeast Asian heritage of the Vietnamese.

Chapter Nine

The Influence of
the Middle East and Europe

The Advent of Islam

From the fourteenth century onward, new forces came out of the West, first from the Middle East, and later from Europe, which deeply affected the ideas and habits of Southeast Asians. Well before the fourteenth century an occasional Muslim trader had found his way eastward to the Malay peninsula or to the islands of the archipelago, but the new religion had to be firmly established in India before it could effectively spread further eastward. The port of Cambay in Gujerat on the west coast of India had long sent traders to Southeast Asia. In the thirteenth century Gujerat fell under Muslim rule, and soon Gujerati Muslims came to Southeast Asia as merchants. As Indians, they must have fitted in more naturally with local life than the occasional Arab merchant who had come earlier, for Southeast Asians had long been accustomed to Indian travelers and merchants, and they were in the habit not only of doing business with them but also of recognizing India as a source of religious inspiration. Just as their Hindu and Buddhist predecessors had done, these Muslim traders often married local women and then raised their children in their own religion.

The crucial step in bringing Islam to Southeast Asia was the conversion of the ruler of Malacca, a city on the west coast of the Malay peninsula, one hundred twenty miles northwest of Singapore. After the year 1400, Malacca assumed an increasingly important role as a trading center. The straits of Malacca, which lie between the Malay peninsula and the island of Sumatra, act as a funnel through which every ship from the west must pass on its way to the archipelago, to the Spice Islands or to China. Whoever controls the straits can dominate the sea trade between East and West and, with skillful management, can grow wealthy and powerful. Strategic and commercial control of the straits had long been a goal of the competing powers of the area, and Malacca rose to dominance in the fifteenth century. Its rulers, at first little more than pirates, forced an increasing number of ships to put into their port. Traders settled in the town and goods were bought and sold, until gradually the older powers were forced to recognize Malacca as the chief port of transit between the Spice Islands and India.

At that time China, under the early Ming Dynasty, was passing through one of her expansionist and imperialistic phases. She sent naval expeditions as far as the east coast of Africa and, in 1403, a roving Chinese fleet visited Malacca. Soon China, too, recognized her position, and for many decades the rulers of Malacca acknowledged no suzerainty but that of China. By sending periodic tribute, Malacca gained China's protection against the Thai who had been their most powerful competitors in the peninsula. China, in turn, prevented any single state from becoming so powerful as to threaten her own supremacy. The rulers of Malacca gradually spread their control from the city to the surrounding countryside and even across the straits to Sumatra, but their control of land was uncertain, and they never became masters of any sizable territory. Their power was always based instead upon the dominance of a single strategic port and the control of trade which resulted.

Into the port of Malacca came nutmeg from the Banda Islands, cloves from the Moluccas, pepper from Sumatra and West Java, camphor and gold from Sumatra, sandalwood from Timor. Many of these were transshipped at Malacca and carried to India and, from there, to Europe. Back from India came textiles—Bengal cotton and Cambay cloth, much of it produced in centers catering specifically to Southeast Asian tastes. Indian ships also brought opium from Arabia, and wool, hats, glass beads, and metal products from the Mediterranean. Silk, satin, damask, and brocade came from China, as did porcelain, pearls, and silver. The teak forests of Burma were tapped to build ships and Malayan mines produced the tin from which the Malaccan coins were minted. Rice was imported from Java and Burma, and Java also sent fruit, vegetables, fish, and meat, for Malacca—with its energies concentrated upon commerce—was not even self-sufficient in food. Ships from as far away as Arabia and China visited the city, bringing their goods, trading, and carrying away new loads for the return trip. Like Singapore at a later date, Malacca stood at the hub of the trade lines which reached out in all directions.

Muslims became established very early in northern Sumatran ports across the straits from Malacca, and during the first quarter of the fifteenth century the ruler of Malacca married the daughter of the Sultan of one of these ports and agreed to become a Muslim. His successors continued to bear Hindu titles but, from that time onward, Malacca became the chief center for the further propagation of Islam.

Malaccan merchants set up shop in many of the ports to the east, and most of these merchants were Muslims. The rulers of the trading ports supported each other and consolidated their own power by exchanging wives and thus forming political alliances. A Muslim ruler would give his sister or daughter only to another Muslim, and so an increasing number of the ruling families were brought into Islam, and Muslim sultanates became established along the coasts wherever trade was important. The sultanates, like Malacca, based their strength upon trade and were little concerned with control over territory. Islam did spread inland from these centers to the general population, but in modern Indonesia Islam is still strongest in the ports and among the trading classes. Older ceremonial forms continue among the farmers and among the descendants of the old nobility though most people now express at least a nominal allegiance to Islam. The new religion brought its requirements for prayer and fasting, though these have been liberally interpreted in Malaya and Indonesia, and it brought an identification with a worldwide movement symbolized by the pilgrimage to Mecca, the goal of all faithful Muslims. Islam also brought the Arabic alphabet which displaced older Indian alphabets in Malaya and the islands.

Islam closely followed the trade routes to the Spice Islands, and the mainland to the north was largely bypassed. Perhaps a people already devoted to a vigorous Buddhist tradition were well equipped to resist the preachings of a new religion but, in any event, the mainland was away from the main lines of trade. Islam did penetrate to the Chams, descendants of the people of ancient

Champa, who were finally conquered by the Vietnamese in 1470. When the Chams became Muslims, they acquired a curious cultural link with the island people, for not only are they the only sizable Malao-Polynesian-speaking people north of Malaya, but they became the largest Muslim group there as well.

The First Europeans

Malacca had but a short period of independence, for new powers were gathering in the West. A few Europeans had already traveled through the straits of Malacca. The most famous was Marco Polo, who passed by on his return from China in 1297. He and others gave Europeans a far clearer knowledge of the rest of the world than they had previously had, particularly with regard to the sources of their precious spices. The hope of reaching the sources directly, and so avoiding the need to buy through Arab and Indian middlemen, became a chief goal of the voyages of the Age of Discovery.

By the fifteenth century the Portuguese were exploring the west coast of Africa, and in 1487 Diaz rounded the Cape of Good Hope. A decade later, ships under Vasco de Gama reached Calicut on the west coast of India, loaded spices, and returned to Europe around the Cape. Now the full possibilities of the trade were revealed, but to exploit it fully, the Portuguese first had to defeat the Muslims in the Arabian Sea. They turned to this task with enthusiasm, for they saw their fight as a continuation of their wars with the Moors that had only recently cleared the Iberian peninsula of Muslim power. By 1510 the Portuguese had taken Goa on the west coast of India and established themselves as the dominant sea power. A Portuguese fleet first visited Malacca in 1508, and in 1511 Portugal captured the city. For another century Malacca continued its dominance in trade, for the Portuguese made it their headquarters although they also established outposts in the Spice Islands. Portugal had achieved her goal of linking the opposite ends of the spice route and circumventing the middlemen. To reach western Europe, spices had formerly passed successively through Malaccan, Indian, Arab, and Venetian hands; now the Portuguese could carry them in a single journey. The wealth that flowed to Portugal was great, but the risks were also high. Every man who sailed eastward gambled on never returning, for many died in combat or of disease, but the success of those who did return encouraged others to follow, and other nations soon looked enviously upon the Portuguese triumph. Spanish ships crossed the Pacific to reach the Spice Islands, and Dutch and English adventurers soon began to take an interest as well.

At the end of the sixteenth century European power was shifting northward from the Iberian peninsula to England and Holland, a shift that has been symbolized to countless schoolchildren by the British defeat of the Spanish Armada in 1588. Dutch ships had been carrying spices northward from Lisbon, and a few Dutch sailors had visited the Moluccas as crew members on Portuguese ships. In 1595 a Dutch fleet left for the Spice Islands, returning home with spices in 1597. In spite of the fact that only 89 men returned of the 249 who started on this voyage, the voyage was considered such a resounding success that new expeditions were quickly prepared.

The Dutch established bases in Java and allied themselves with local princes who had become enemies of the Portuguese. The Dutch then fought the Portuguese for control of shipping and, after several unsuccessful attempts and a long blockade and siege, they finally captured Malacca in 1641. This ended Malacca's period of commercial dominance, for the center of trade shifted to the Dutch settlement at Batavia (now Jakarta), in Java. For the next two centuries the Dutch were the chief European power in Southeast Asia. The Portuguese clung to Timor and the Spanish were established in the Philippines. The British poured their energies into their growing Indian empire, and it was not until the early nineteenth century that they established themselves firmly in Malaya. Even the Dutch only very slowly extended their rule inland from their Javanese coastal bases.

By the middle of the nineteenth century, Southeast Asia had undergone three centuries of direct European intervention, but these centuries brought few changes to the life of the indigenous people. Like the Indians and the Chinese who had preceded them, the Europeans settled primarily along the coast. They found commerce thriving, and it proved possible to seize control of a few strategic centers and then operate as other traders had been doing for centuries. To the indigenous people, these new arrivals could not have appeared so greatly different from the tradesmen and ambassadors who had been coming from India and China for so long. Their numbers were never large and their technical superiority was not great, though their guns and their knowledge of geography and navigation gave them a critical advantage. Fortunately for the Europeans, Southeast Asians were themselves divided and some were as eager for European allies as the Europeans were for local bases. During the first three centuries of European contact, power was by no means monopolized by the foreigners: Europeans controlled the major shipping routes and international trade but hardly any sizable piece of territory, even in the islands. Local rulers continued in power; they allied themselves with Europeans when it seemed advantageous and they, too, profited from the spice trade.

To the north, where the lure of trade was less, European contact was even more superficial. European weapons found their way to local armies so that the battles could become even more bloody than before. Portuguese mercenaries fought for the Burmese as early as 1541 and other European adventurers occasionally hired themselves out to the service of Thai and Burmese rulers. From time to time, European ambassadors visited the various courts and a few transient attempts were made to establish trading centers along the coast of the mainland. The mainland powers, however, did not depend upon control of the shipping lanes, and they pursued their old rivalries with undiminished vigor.

In the sixteenth century the new Toungoo dynasty brought renewed unity to fragmented Burma and forthwith began a long and exhausting rivalry with the Thai. The Thai at the same time continued to fight the Cambodians, and the Vietnamese pressed their southward expansion. By the end of the seventeenth century the Vietnamese had fully absorbed old Champa, but conflict between north and south did not cease, for the ruling families of Annam and Tonkin competed for dominance among the Vietnamese. The almost incessant wars among the Southeast Asian states discouraged European trade, but throughout the sixteenth, seventeenth, and eighteenth centuries little on the mainland really attracted the Europeans. Slowly—through ambassadors, merchants, and adventurers—a growing knowledge of the rest of the world and some control over its weapons seeped into Southeast Asia, but for three centuries Europeans had dabbled in the complex rivalries of Southeast Asian politics, but had gained no decisive advantage.

The Later Colonial Period

Quite naturally European colonialism has become the whipping boy of resurgent Southeast Asian nationalism, but European dominance was actually confined to the last century of the four hundred years of European contact. The new and radical form of colonialism was the child of the Industrial Revolution, which brought changes to Europe even more rapidly than to other parts of the world. As the first to exploit the new industrial techniques, the European nations had a decisive though temporary advantage in the struggle for power. For a single century the changes brought by industrial development were organized and led by Europeans, in Southeast Asia as in the rest of the world. From 1850 onward, local Southeast Asian trade could be conducted more profitably by steamship than by the older sailing ships and Chinese junks. After 1870 steamships came to dominate the traffic between Europe and Asia. In 1869 the Suez Canal opened, shortening the distance between Europe and Asia and making trade more profitable and less risky. In 1865 the first telegraph lines between Europe and India were opened, and in succeeding years they were extended eastward. For the first time, the home countries could exercise day-to-day direction over their far-flung dependencies. Developing European industries required raw materials. Tin and rubber from Malaya were demanded in ever-increasing quantities. Burma became the world's leading producer of tungsten, Asia's leading producer of silver and lead, and the site of a modest but profitable petroleum industry. And, in return, the industries of Europe showered Southeast Asia with an ever-growing supply of manufactured goods.

The new forms of transportation and communication facilitated the incorporation of Southeast Asian territory into European colonial systems, and the need for both raw materials and markets made such incorporation seem desirable to a growing number of people in the home countries.

For many years the British government in India tried to establish an orderly relationship with the Burmese kings who were established near Mandalay. Mandalay is in upper Burma, far from the sea coast, and far from effective contact with foreign powers. In this remote location the Burmese rulers further isolated themselves behind such ceremonial pomp that they were shielded from a realistic knowledge of European strength. It is difficult to know who was sillier, the occasional British envoy who refused to follow the local courtesy of removing his shoes in the presence of the Burmese king, or the Burmese who arrogantly declined to deal with the representative of the mere Viceroy in India, when they felt that as leaders of a sovereign power they should properly deal only with the direct representative of the British queen. In any event, the Burmese badly miscalculated the strength of the British, and it was to require many decades of conflict before the realities of the new situation penetrated to the Burmese rulers—and by then it was too late to salvage independence.

Burma had sacked Ayuthia, the capital of Thailand, in 1767, and tried to repeat its performance in 1785. This time, however, the Burmese suffered a serious defeat, and in succeeding decades they turned increasingly covetous eyes in the opposite direction, toward the independent states which lay between Burma and British Bengal. A series of border incidents continually aggravated relationships between the British and Burma. In 1817 the Burmese invaded Assam, which, unlike Bengal, was still independent of Britain. By 1822 they completed their conquest, and it appeared that Burma was making serious plans to invade Bengal. The British now took strong counteraction, and the first Burmese war began. By 1826 Burma was humiliated into surrendering Assam, Manipur, Arakan, and Tenasserim to the British, and was required to pay a large indemnity besides. The British hoped that this would end Burmese truculence, but though the defeat wounded, it did not still Burmese pride. Relations remained hopelessly strained until the second and third Burmese wars, which followed at thirty-year intervals. In 1852 lower Burma, and in 1886 the last independent territory of upper Burma, were annexed by the British. Step by step, and with seemingly inexorable momentum, British power had extended eastward from its Indian bastions, until all Burma was incorporated into the Indian Empire.

During the same period, France was carving out an empire on the opposite side of the Southeast Asian peninsula. France's interest was first aroused by missionaries who, as early as the seventeenth century, had worked in what was later to become French Indo-China. They had met with varying degrees of friendship and enmity, but in the 1830's and 1840's opposition to the missionaries increased, and local authorities went so far as to execute a few of them. By 1843, however, France was for the first time in a position to intervene directly; at gun point she demanded the release of five condemned missionaries. This was the period during which many European nations were demanding and obtaining special rights for their subjects in China, and France was simply extending protection to her nationals in Vietnam as well. Like the Burmese, however, the Vietnamese misjudged the power of the Europeans, and they continued to harass French nationals dwelling in their territory at the very moment when France was looking for an excuse to invade. When her demands for the safety of French nationals and her request for permission to establish diplomatic stations were rejected, the French armies marched. In 1862 the eastern part of Cochin-China (as the southern part of Vietnam was then called) was occupied; five years later the western part was overcome. In 1867 the Thai were forced to relinquish their claim to suzerainty over Cambodia and to recognize the French position. Hanoi, in northern Vietnam, was seized in 1882 and, after a short war, France obtained China's recognition of her position and sealed her claim to all Vietnam. Finally, in 1893, a protectorate over Laos was declared and the French empire in Asia was complete.

Thailand was situated uneasily between the expanding spheres of British and French interest and had been forced to cede some territorial claims to each, but Thailand had two decisive advantages over the Burmese and Vietnamese. On the one hand, the Thai rulers were far more astute in their judgment of European power. Their capital was in the south, where they had long and continuous experience with European visitors. They avoided the mistake of underestimating them. For the most part Thailand carefully refrained from incidents which might have provoked direct European intervention. On the other hand, as France and Britain advanced toward each other from opposite sides of the peninsula, the two powers grew mutually suspicious and neither was inclined to let the other seize the last remaining neutral zone between them. Little Thailand became a buffer between the two great European powers, both of whom finally came to respect her territorial integrity. At the same time Thailand did not fail to modernize her administration and economy. Avoiding self-defeating chauvinism, Thailand hired European specialists for the government services and sent her own citizens abroad to learn Western techniques. Peaceful merchants from many countries were permitted to visit the country, but the Thai avoided letting any single nation gain a predominant commercial position. As a result, the political and commercial development of Thailand kept pace with that of her neighbors, and she eventually emerged as the only Southeast Asian nation with the experience of uninterrupted self-rule. Ironically, the absence of foreign domination has made the Thai cling less tenaciously to symbols of the past than have their neighbors. Western clothing, for instance, has been adopted more readily in Thailand than elsewhere in Southeast Asia. Superficially, at least, the only Southeast Asian nation which was never a European colony is as Westernized as any of its neighbors.

Colonial Power: Consolidation and Expansion

Elsewhere in Asia, Europeans capitalized upon their temporary technological superiority and everywhere they seemed to be destined to lead. British power was consolidated in India; Japan was opened up; and China forced to grant special privileges to Europeans. The Philippine Islands, after three centuries of Spanish rule, were taken over by the United States. In the 1870's and 1880's, the sultanates of Malaya gradually accepted British guidance as British power spread inland from the older coastal settlements of Singapore, Malacca, and Penang. Dutch rule spread over all Indonesia. By the early 1890's, the division of territory was complete. For the next fifty years European rule brought a temporary halt to the internal rivalries of Southeast Asia, while the local people learned enough of the ideas and technology of their European masters to reach once more for independence.

In the end, it was to be those same European doctrines and techniques that would be turned against the conquerors and used to send them back across the sea. In nineteenth-century Europe the gospel of nationalism had inspired and given moral sanction to colonial expansion. Europeans came to Asia not only to grow wealthy but to build the "glory" of their fatherlands. It could not be long before the conquered people caught the nationalist fervor of their masters and, applying it to their own case, used it to inspire resistance and revolt. Once the Japanese victories at the beginning of World War II demonstrated that the new techniques of war could be turned against their European inventors, the fate of colonialism was sealed.

Peaceful conditions and systematic colonial rule made possible the expanding commerce that the new industries of Europe required. Earlier trade in Southeast Asia consisted of compact but valuable cargo such as spices and precious metals, but bulk cargo now became economically profitable. In the deltas of Burma, Thailand, Cambodia, and southern Vietnam, the commercial production of rice began to climb rapidly. During the period just before the arrival of the Europeans, the deltas had been only sparsely populated, but in each country settlers soon began arriving from the more densely populated north. Homesteaders cleared the jungle and built the irrigation and drainage systems that were needed to turn the deltas into the rice padis. Millions of new acres of land came under cultivation: by the 1930's French Indo-China was exporting 1.5 million tons of rice annually; Thailand, 2 million; and Burma 3.5 million. Rice flowed to India, Ceylon, Malaya, China, and Japan to help feed their rapidly expanding populations.

Because this new agriculture grew in response to a new market rather than to the subsistence needs of the population, most of the surplus rice crop in the deltas has always been sold. The farmers in the new lands worked in a completely monetary economy and became subject to all the vagaries of fluctuating prices. Few ordinary farmers ever had sufficient capital to get themselves started on a sound financial footing and in every country land tended to fall into the control of moneylenders or absentee landowners. The proportion of tenancy has been much higher in the southern deltas than in the older farming areas of the north, and the turnover of tenants has been high. Absentee landlords and impermanent tenants combine to let long-term care of the land be sacrificed for immediate profits. Tenants who feel they have no stake in the future of the land, and who feel themselves to be exploited by their creditors, provide poor material for a peaceful national development. (This may help to explain the peculiar situation in prewar Burma, which had the highest rate of violent crime of any part of British India.) Impermanence, shallow ties with neighbors, and dependence upon cash crops all discourage the older and more traditional patterns of labor exchange and mutual assistance. Farm labor is more likely to be paid for in impersonal cash than with reciprocal labor, and the money economy of the world market reaches clear down to affect the relationship between neighbors.

Low wages and the peculiar problems of wet rice agriculture have discouraged mechanization, except that mills prepare most commercial rice and even much of the rice destined for local use, but new and more efficient means of transportation now carry the rice from the farms to world markets. The rivers continue to handle much of the freight, but canals, railroads, and motor roads, have come to supplement the river traffic. Today trucks and buses tie the farmer more intimately to the trade centers than ever before.

Minerals and forest products have played a poor second to rice as a source of foreign exchange, but all have contributed to the ability of Southeast Asians to import the products of the rest of the world. Mill cloth, hats, umbrellas, bicycles, needles, safety pins, scissors, playing cards, pencils, pens, razor blades, mirrors, hair oil, aspirin, and penicillin have flooded Southeast Asian markets and changed Southeast Asian tastes. Few of these goods are yet manufactured in Southeast Asia, but as technological knowledge spreads, mill cloth from India, flashlight batteries from Hong Kong, cameras from Japan, and thousands of rubber and cloth shoes from Malaya are added to the list of European and American imports, contributing new wealth and inspiring new longings. Trucks, electric generators, locomotives, and airplanes arrive in increasing numbers. Even in remote Laos, the consumer reaps the first rewards of the Industrial Revolution as he becomes accustomed to matches, printed newspapers and bottled soft drinks at the same time that he suffers the effects of the Industrial Revolution's weapons.

As imported manufactured goods become more readily available, older crafts inevitably decline. When mill cloth can be cheaply purchased, women gladly give up their weaving. The kerosene tin replaces the beautiful but fragile earthenware pot for storing water, rubber shoes replace wooden clogs, and trucks replace oxcarts. The logic of industrialization is to encourage specialization in the product that each area or each man can produce best, and in Southeast Asia it is most profitable to produce rice and exchange it for the goods of other areas.

Even as older crafts disappear, new skills appear. Truckdrivers, mechanics, and mill workers are needed, as are merchants to collect the rice and distribute the manufactured goods. Many more government officials to supervise the new and more complex economic organization, and more teachers to pass on the expanded knowledge, become essential to the new way of life. The expanded scale of trade, together with the increased role of the government, encourages the growth of cities and towns, and this growth has brought one exception to the pattern of single crop agriculture: around the cities, truck gardening has become increasingly profitable. Instead of specializing in rice, a few farmers specialize in vegetables, and near Rangoon, whole farms are devoted to flowers which are trucked to the city and sold.

As Europeans drew Southeast Asians into the political and economic network that would bind them to the West, an attempt was also made to bring them Western religion. The Protestants neatly divided up this corner of the world: Baptists were assigned the task of saving the people of Burma and most of Assam; Thailand fell to the Presbyterians; the French colonies, to the Christian and Missionary Alliance; Malaya, to the Methodists; and the bordering parts of China, to the China Inland Mission. Roman Catholics and the more fundamentalist Protestant sects could never recognize such jurisdictional boundaries and each extended its work as widely as possible.

The missionaries invented alphabets, encouraged literacy, printed books, founded hospitals, taught elementary techniques of sanitation, built schools, and spread Western education, but they had only limited successes in persuading Southeast Asians of the truth of their assorted doctrines. Most of their potential flock were already committed to subtle religious doctrines with well-tested philosophical foundations, and as nationalist ideas spread, the older religions came to be not only spiritual systems but symbols of national pride as well. One of the earliest centers of developing Burmese nationalism was the Young Men's Buddhist Association, modeled upon its Christian counterpart but Buddhist and nationalistic in its inspirations. Christianity came to be regarded by many Southeast Asians as just another tool of Western imperialism. The limited areas in which Christianity was relatively successful were often those where minorities were developing their own local nationalism. For them, Christianity sometimes became a symbol which stood for their separation from the majority of their country's population: In Burma, two thirds of the Christians are said to be Karens, one of the largest minorities of southern Burma; in Assam, a large proportion of the tribal people have become Christians, and they cite their new religion as the most distinctive mark of their separate identity. Instead of serving to build universal brotherhood, Christianity has been used by Southeast Asians to reinforce old divisions.

Through political conquest, commerce, and the new Western style of education, Southeast Asians came to be far more dependent upon the rest of the world than ever before. The products of Western industries were eagerly sought, but the assumption of Western superiority was resented and rejected. Southeast Asians absorbed the technological skill and the forms and vocabulary of Western political idealogies and even the end of direct Western rule could never reverse the accelerating integration of Southeast Asia into the rest of the world. The forces set in motion by the Industrial Revolution were not dependent upon colonialism. Western rule marked only the first step of the integration; it could not outlast the ability of the rest of the world to grasp the techniques which had given the West its initial but temporary advantage.

Chapter Ten

Chinese and Indian Immigration

The Chinese

Far from interrupting the long-established relazionship between Southeast Asia and India and China, the period of colonial
rule actually enhanced it. Before World War II, there was no independent Indian government, and the Chinese government was too
weak to compete directly with Europeans in Southeast Asia, but immigrants came from both countries and settled widely. As a result,
over 10 per cent, or about three million, of Thailand's people are
Chinese (if locally born Chinese are included, nearly half of the
people of Bangkok were ethnically Chinese in 1954, and in the center of the city the population was overwhelmingly Chinese); one
million of Burma's are of Indian origin. South Vietnam has 800,000
Chinese; Cambodia, 250,000; and, even excluding predominantly
(85 per cent) Chinese Singapore, 2.5 million of Malaya's 6.5 million people are Chinese and another 700,000 are Indians.

Although the quest for wealth and the flight from oppression at
home have long brought Chinese and Indians to Southeast Asia,
never—until the last hundred years—have they come in such large
numbers. To the crowded poor of India and China, the relatively
open spaces of Southeast Asia have beckoned as a frontier where the
poor man could hope to find riches and return home a wealthy
man. Thousands have traveled to this frontier; not a few have succeeded in amassing the fortune and returning home as planned.
Others have stayed in their new homes, either because they failed to
acquire the wealth to return to their old ones or because they became too deeply committed to their new lives abroad, but more
than is the case among European immigrants in America, Indian
and Chinese immigrants who stayed in Southeast Asia have retained
their attachment to their native countries. Because they have often

been slow to adopt the customs of their new surroundings, distinctive foreign minorities have grown up within every Southeast Asian nation. The immigrants always form an energetic, ambitious minority, and they have made vital contributions to the development of the Southeast Asian economy, but their very success has evoked the jealousy of the indigenous people.

More immigrants have come from China than from India—most of them from two provinces of the southern Chinese coast: Kwantung and Fukien. For centuries, Chinese junks have traveled between these provinces and the ports of Southeast Asia. Conditions in the latter half of the nineteenth century permitted more intensive contact and encouraged migration. At that time, just as the peace of the late colonial era was coming to Southeast Asia, China was entering a period of political instability. The surge of world trade brought a new demand for labor in Southeast Asia and Chinese migrated southward to work on the docks and in the mills, to build railroads, to mine tin, and later to man the rubber plantations. A man with a sense for commerce could profit by participating in the increasingly widespread trade both in farm crops and in manufactured goods. In brief, the same forces that drew the European powers to take an increasing interest in Southeast Asia also made it attractive to the Chinese, but unlike the Europeans, the Chinese had to come with little protection from their government. China was so beset by internal political turmoil that its government could take little direct action overseas, and its citizens had to seek their fortunes as individuals.

Most of the early Chinese immigrants were men. Some had left wives behind in China but many married local women. Neither racial differences nor, in Buddhist countries, religious differences stood in the way of intermarriage, and intermarriage served gradually to draw the Chinese men, and especially their children, into the life of their new country. As long as migration was largely confined to men and as long as their numbers remained small in proportion to the indigenous population, they and their children were gradually assimilated to local ways. Inevitably the children learned their mother's language, and—if having a foreign father made any difference at all—it served only to inculcate in the chil-

dren an ethic of hard work and individual initiative. Many of today's most prominent Southeast Asian leaders are able to trace at
least a fraction of their ancestry to China.

After World War I, however, a growing proportion of women
were included among the immigrants. Men brought their wives or
sent back for them after they had established themselves in the new
land. This may have been a sign of greater willingness to settle
down in their adopted country, but it also created a Chinese community far less vulnerable to assimilation. Inevitably, Chinese
women set up Chinese-style households, and the children they raised
acquired sentiments which were oriented more toward the country
of their parents' birth than to that of their own. Particularly in the
cities, where the Chinese have always concentrated in the greatest
numbers, the children could grow up in almost undiluted Chinese
surroundings.

It has been estimated that before World War I, no more than one
tenth of the Chinese population of Thailand were women. Between
the wars, however, the proportion of women among the immigrants
gradually climbed to about one third of the total, and when the locally born are included, the sex ratio among the Chinese has even begun to approach normality since World War II. In Singapore, too,
the proportion of women climbed steadily from 18 per cent in 1911
to 44 per cent in 1947, and this no doubt reflects conditions elsewhere in Southeast Asia. Intermarriage between Chinese men and
local women has grown correspondingly rare.

Several languages are spoken in Kwantung and Fukien, the home
provinces of most of the immigrants, and while these are usually referred to as "dialects" because the speakers use the same written
language, they are mutually unintelligible. As a result, speakers of a
half-dozen different speech groups have shared in the migration
southward: Cantonese from Kwantung, Hainanese from the island
of Hainan off the coast, Teochui from the vicinity of Swatow in
northern Kwantung, Hokkien from Fukien, and Hakkas from parts
of both provinces. More of the immigrants came from farming villages than from cities, but their villages were not a poor prepara-
tion for the urban life which so many adopted in Southeast Asia.
The shift from farmer to craftsman, peddler or petty trader, was not
difficult in China, and every farmer had to be something of a jack-

of-all-trades. Traditional village crafts, such as carpentry, could be readily used in the new home, and Chinese villagers had for centuries been accustomed to a thoroughgoing monetary economy. The buying and selling of labor, of crops, and of the products of handicraft were part of the traditions of even the most remote Chinese villages.

More than any Southeast Asians, the Chinese subordinated women to their husbands. A new wife usually had to live with her husband's family for a few years at least—often directed by a domineering mother-in-law and always playing a subservient role. In southern China a woman almost always had to leave her native village at marriage and live among the strangers of her husband's village. Ancestor worship was directed toward those in the paternal line; a woman's children honored her husband's ancestors, not her own. Houses united by descent from the same male ancestor formed a clan which, in theory at least, was led by the oldest male member of the senior generation. Factors other than seniority alone influenced a man's prestige and his ability to assert effective leadership, however, and the possibility of social mobility had never been completely absent in China. Farmers could become petty traders, and able traders occasionally turned into prosperous merchants. Skillful handling of business and adroit manipulation of capital might make possible the education of a son who could sit for and conceivably pass the state examinations. The government bureaucracy was staffed by successful examinees. Several generations might lie between the farmer and the government official, but an ambitious man could at least conceive the idea of improving his social rank. Even the first step in the process—the acquisition of wealth—brought a measure of influence within the clan and the village that could override the seniority of another kinsman.

Villagers in traditional China had but limited contact with the central government. They paid taxes, sometimes in money, sometimes in the form of labor, and in principle they received a degree of security and a minimum of public works in return, but the lowest rung of the central government reached only to the district capital, and the more wealthy and better educated village men served as the link between the bureaucracy above and the farmer below. These men tried to use their influence to prevent internal village disputes from incurring bureaucratic interference, and under the turbulent conditions of southeastern China during the nineteenth century, men often had to look to their kinsmen and their fellow villagers for mutual help and protection. The ordinary village hoped for little from the government other than to be left alone.

It was from these villages that the immigrants came. They brought their skill in the use of money, a faith in the possibility of individual social mobility through the acquisition of wealth, a long tradition of hard work, the ideal of male dominance in the family and in business, and always an intense loyalty both to the village where their ancestors lay buried and to the larger and more abstract Chinese civilization of which they might have little sophisticated understanding but to which they knew they somehow belonged. Some came independently, but others were recruited for specific jobs. The immigrants were often poverty-stricken and indentured for the price of their passages southward, but they were hard-working and ambitious, and their skills were badly needed in Southeast Asia. Not all became rich, but a few amassed fortunes and created rags-to-riches legends which can match those of any other part of the world.

The economic niche that the Chinese were uniquely qualified to fill was that of middleman between the indigenous farmers and the new economic machine that the Industrial Revolution was creating in the West. European firms in Southeast Asia could import the new manufactured goods, but they needed a way to distribute them to the countryside, and they needed to collect the farmers' surplus rice for export. Native Southeast Asians were in a poor position to help. The success of Thai and Burmese women in the marketing of local produce should dispel any notion of a mysterious superior Chinese aptitude for business, but local men had not traditionally been accustomed to spend all day in a shop. Moreover, it was difficult for a Burmese or Thai villager to learn enough about the characteristics of the markets and the availability of goods. His own roots usually lay in a village and he lacked personal acquaintance with the urban wholesalers who would be his suppliers. If he overcame all this and began to make a success of his business, he was still in danger of being besieged by jealous kinsmen, forced to give bad loans or to hire unneeded help. Although the Chinese also relied upon each other for help, they at least granted to the individual merchant the right to plan his own business affairs. Needy kinsmen were thousands of miles away, and if he were called upon to help another Chinese, a merchant could also expect help in return. For all these reasons Chinese shopkeepers have established themselves over most of Southeast Asia as the economic link between the farmer and the rest of the world. The farmer sells his grain to one Chinese merchant, and he buys his cloth and thread, cooking pots, soap, kerosene, hardware, and bicycles from others. He hires a Chinese carpenter to build his house, and takes his family to eat in a Chinese restaurant. Tanning, butchering, sugarmaking, lumbering, and even weaving, are all likely to be in Chinese hands.

A few Southeast Asian Chinese have been able to rise from their small businesses and to succeed in areas that were once dominated by Europeans. Not only local inns, but large modern hotels are often Chinese-owned and operated. Insurance, shipping, banking, heavy construction, and even motion picture production all have Chinese participation. Many Chinese remain poor and far more are modest shopkeepers than are financial moguls, but the evidence of flourishing Chinese enterprise is visible everywhere in Southeast Asia today.

A few Chinese shops are found in almost every town, and Chinese peddlers visit even remote villages. Where Chinese are most concentrated, their occupations are most varied. In Malaya, where their numbers are highest, Chinese work rubber plantations, mine tin, and even farm, but whether in an urban metropolis or in a small provincial town, the most characteristic occupation of Chinese in Southeast Asia today is shopkeeping.

The typical Chinese shop is a family concern, and the living quarters of the family merge physically with the business area of the shop, just as the family life and business merge in the affairs of the people. The public room of the shop opens out onto the street. At night, it can be boarded shut, but during the day it is opened in front for its full width, so that the noise and commotion of the public street flow into the shop. The goods to be sold are piled about, and customers drift in and out to be waited on by the proprietor, his wife, or—if it is a fairly large shop—a hired clerk. Even unrelated employees usually eat their meals in the shop with the family and they often sleep there as well. The children of the family help too, by running errands and later, since they are often more literate than their immigrant parents, by keeping the records. They grow up surrounded by buying and selling and learn the skills of the trader at an early age.

Behind and above the public room are the family's private quarters. The kitchen is likely to be on the ground floor and the men usually eat in the shop at the traditional round table, in full view of the passersby on the street. Bedrooms are above. When married sons live at home, each must have a separate room where he, his wife, and their small children sleep, and in a large family, her bedroom is the only place where a daughter-in-law can escape from her husband's relatives and find privacy. However, no more than in China is the ideal of keeping the sons together in a large family uniformly met, for limitations of space often force sons to move out to their own houses.

The shop not only separates the public street from the family's private rooms, it also separates the world of men from the world of women. Chinese women are free to come and go on daily errands, but their first duty is always in the home, where they care for the children, cook the family's meals, and attentively wait upon the needs of the men. They sometimes help in the shop, but that is the special responsibility of the men, and business relationships outside the shop are almost exclusively conducted by men. Inevitably, it is the men who deal with the non-Chinese nationals of the country and it is the men who must make the greater adjustments to local customs. This is symbolized by the Western clothing that Chinese men, in most parts of Southeast Asia, have long used for business purposes. The women usually show their conservatism by wearing the traditional loose Chinese jacket and trousers. Men are more likely to gain competence or fluency in the language of the host country or in Chinese dialects other than their own. When a woman leaves her home, it is generally only to see other Chinese women, especially if she lives in a city. Inevitably, she runs a Chinese-style home, and children receive their first training in this Chinese setting. The dialect of their parents becomes their first language, and the first etiquette and values they learn are Chinese. When they learn the local language and customs, they learn them as foreigners, and if their learning occurs at a younger age and is therefore more effective than that of their parents, they are still likely to think and act first according to their earliest training and only secondarily according to the traditions of their adopted country.

Education, which has done so much to turn the children of European immigrants into Americans, has worked less well in Southeast Asia. No nation has been rich enough to establish a universal public school system or to insist that all children attend. The Chinese have probably been more aware of the advantages of education than most other people, and have frequently supported their own schools, but in these schools the aim has as often been to give a distinctively Chinese education as to integrate children into the host country. Textbooks have been imported from China, often carrying propaganda for either the Chinese Nationalisits or the Communists. The setting of the goals for, and the direction of the education of Chinese children has been one of the most sensitive issues among Southeast Asian Chinese, and a frequent point of friction with the local governments, for everyone has recognized its importance for the future character of the Chinese community.

The Chinese have brought with them their unique assemblage of religious ideas. Buddhism is important enough to serve as a link with local beliefs, and although urban Chinese in those Southeast Asian countries which adhere to the Therevada doctrine rarely support the local monasteries or enter their children in the monkhood, they do visit local religious shrines and usually respect the ideals of Southern Buddhism. Chinese also continue to practice some of the rituals by which they traditionally show respect to their ancestors. Most households maintain an "ancestor shelf," on which are kept incense and food, but ancestor tablets of recent generations (which in China are usually kept in the home) are more often placed in a Chinese temple. The ancestors themselves lie buried in their village at home. Many Chinese have hoped to return home to die, but even those who have died overseas have sometimes had their remains shipped back after death to join those of their forefathers.

Though the overseas Chinese family—with its explicit male dominance, its equal inheritance by male offspring, and its expectation that women will move to join their husbands—is much like the family in the home country, it has been impossible to recreate the ties which have traditionally bound families together into clans. In southeastern China, households which traced their origin from a common ancestor were joined in clans. Too few generations of Chinese have lived in Southeast Asia for clans to form there, so that the lineage of an overseas Chinese remains located in his home village. Because they can no longer rely upon their distant kinsmen and fellow villagers for help, Southeast Asian Chinese have substituted associations based on principles other than kinship or native village, but serving many of the same purposes. The associations have helped to set the new immigrant on his feet in a strange land, and given settlers a way of channeling mutual assistance. They serve as a shield against governments whose regulations have been at best poorly understood and at worst arbitrary and discriminatory, and they provide a means by which successful Chinese may gain the explicit recognition of their compatriots. Some associations are limited to men with the same surname or to those who come from one particular region of China, but some of the most important are open to all who speak the same Chinese dialect. Still other associations admit all who practice a single trade or specialty.

Each association usually has its own building, modest or imposing depending upon the number and the wealth of its members. It is run by a battery of elected directors and a permanent staff. An office in such an association is the chief honor which the Chinese community can confer upon its wealthy and respected members. Those who contribute money to support the association's activities are listed in its reports, and pictures of the most generous contributors are hung in the association building. The officers of the associations amount to a *Who's Who* in the Chinese community.

The explicit purpose of an association is to give aid to its members and service to the community. Government-sponsored welfare programs have been almost nonexistent in the countries of Southeast Asia. Thus, in the new urban setting, the Chinese associations have met many otherwise unfilled needs. They have sponsored schools, supported hospitals, and distributed alms to the poor. One association in Bangkok regularly assists people whose homes or shops have been burned. News of changing governmental regulations, and advice about the best means of coping with them are passed to the members. Although the associations may not formally restrict membership to Chinese, their business is conducted in one or another of the Chinese dialects, and so they are effectively closed to others. This adds to the difficulties faced by a non-Chinese who wishes to enter a business, for the associations serve as one the main sources of business and market information—a source to which the Thai, Malay, or Cambodian has no access. If two people who speak the same dialect have a dispute, their association tries to settle the matter. Even a dispute between an employer and his workers over employment conditions may be settled through the good offices of an association. The Chinese seem not to have lost their old attitude that the less they have to do with the government the less trouble they will have. In these respects the associations fill many of the same needs as the village or the clan back home. There also, through the leadership of the men of wealth and prestige, internal disputes were ironed out and the authority of the government kept at bay. In Thailand the government-like character of the associations has even had a quasilegal basis: the Chinese Chamber of Commerce—the most important of the Bangkok associations—has performed some consular duties, and the Thai government has dealt with the Chamber as the recognized spokesman of the Chinese community.

Economic mobility has surely been far more rapid in Southeast Asia than it could have been in China. Nearly every immigrant was poor when he first arrived, and few could boast of illustrious ancestors. However, illustrious ancestors have never been essential to the socially ambitious Chinese and the mobility of Southeast Asian Chinese has only accentuated an ancient theme of Chinese culture. Mutual assistance has not been lacking among overseas Chinese but, as in China, individual households have been left with the responsibility to work hard and to build their own businesses. Wealth has been the overriding goal of the Chinese immigrants, and it was to gain wealth that they left their homes. Those who have been successful have used part of their money to support their associations and to earn the admiration of their compatriots, but the road to wealth has been through hard individual effort.

In traditional China, wealthy families tried to educate a son to enter the government, but whether under colonial rule or self-government, the bureaucracies in Southeast Asia have been largely closed to the Chinese. Even the large Chinese population of Malaya has been underrepresented in governmental service, and further north few immigrants work for the government. In part, this is because the indigenous people have been unwilling to admit aliens, whose loyalty they consider suspect, to the powers or rewards of government, but in part it is because the Chinese have been unwilling to commit themselves to any particular political regime. Business opportunities have looked far more promising to them than uncertain government posts. Of course, the Chinese community has had to come to terms with the government in power, and individual Chinese merchants have reached formal or informal understandings with members of the government. Large concerns sometimes include an influential official on their board of directors. The firm pays the official well, and he reciprocates by handling its dealings with the government. The arrangement also helps to bypass any laws which attempt to limit alien ownership of firms. Day-to-day direction of the concern is, of course, left in the hands of the Chinese entrepreneur. It is hardly surprising to hear charges of less formal agreements between Chinese merchants and government officials, when one considers the power of officials to help or to harass the business community, and the money with which the business leaders can tempt officialdom to decide matters in their favor.

The position of the overseas Chinese has been complicated by the conflict between the Nationalist and Communist governments of China. The two have competed for the loyalty of the overseas Chinese and community sentiment has often been badly split. Under the circumstances, most Chinese prefer not to take too active a political role. It could prove disastrous to have supported the losing side too vigorously and, in view of the instability of Southeast Asian governments, vociferous support of the one in power might prove a future embarrassment. The only reasonable course has often seemed to be a nonpolitical one, and businessman usually try to steer carefully enough between opposing political credos to be able to do business with whoever is in power. Only in Malaya, through sheer weight of numbers, have the Chinese taken a more active and public role in the government.

The Indians

Indian immigration into Southeast Asia has been less extensive than the Chinese, but in the last century many Indians have fol-

lowed the old trade routes eastward. Because of geographical proximity and common colonial control, Indian migration was concentrated in the British territories of Burma and Malaya. Like their
Chinese contemporaries, the earlier Indian immigrants often married local women. Many of these immigrants were Muslims, and in
both Burma and Thailand small but vigorous Muslim minorities
have developed whose members adhere to the dress, manners, and
langauge of their Southeast Asian mothers, but to the religion of
their Indian fathers.

When the immigrants began to arrive in larger numbers, assimilation became more difficult. Moreover, racial differences and—particularly for the Hindus—religious differences have been more of
a barrier to the assimilation of Indians than to that of the Chinese.
Hindu ideas of purity and pollution have interfered with intermarriage, and caste traditions have probably made it more difficult for
Indians to change occupations and adjust to the new and more varied economic opportunities of Southeast Asia. Thousands of laborers, mostly Tamils from southern India, were recruited for the
burgeoning rubber estates of Malaya (they were considered more
docile workers than the Chinese). But in Malaya, fewer Indians than
Chinese have worked their way into trade or the professions; more
of them have stayed instead in unskilled and menial occupations
which Malays have been unwilling to enter and which Chinese have
fought to escape. The bulk of Indian migration has occurred since
1890, and it has consisted largely of single men, many of whom
eventually return home. Until World War II much of the Indian
population was transient, and if anything, had even stronger roots
in the home country than did the Chinese.

Indian migration has been most important in Burma. Relatively
few Chinese immigrants came to Burma, but Indian soldiers
manned the British regiments that conquered the country and
staffed the offices of the British colonial administration. Because
Burma was an integral part of the Indian empire, no restrictions
were placed on Indian migration there. Like the Chinese elsewhere
in Southeast Asia, Indian immigrants manned the docks, built the
railways, and worked in the rice and timber mills which processed
the country's most important exports. British officials and busi-
nessmen hired Indians as their gardeners, their cooks, and their rick-

shaw pullers. The Indians had one advantage over the Burmese: many had received a British-style education and some instruction in the English language which was needed in government offices. As a result, Rangoon in the years before World War II was an Indian city; Indians outnumbered the Burmese, and Hindustani was the lingua franca.

Burma is the one country of Southeast Asia where Indians rather than Chinese have tended to control retail trade, but the Indians who most seriously affected the lives of the average Burmese farmer were Chettiars, who belonged to a caste of moneylenders and bankers and who came to Burma to carry on their traditional occupation. They found it profitable to lend money to Burmese farmers in the rapidly expanding rice areas of the southern delta. Land was mortgaged as the only available security for the loans, and during the depression of the 1930's it became increasingly difficult for the farmers to repay their debts. As a result, Chettiars came to own a large portion of the land and the farmers were reduced to the status of tenants.

World War II was catastrophic for the Indian community in Burma. As the Japanese invasion became imminent, thousands of Indians fled to their native country. Civil services in Rangoon collapsed, and streams of refugees fought to get out of Burma by every possible route. They went by small boat along the coast, and they walked westward over the mountains into Assam. Suddenly the Indian population dropped and, in particular, most of the Chettiars departed. Burmese farmers happily bid farewell to their creditors and, although the legal issue is a bit obscure, the Burmese farmers have, in effect, been able to act as full owners of the land.

The success of the immigrants in Southeast Asia has caused them to be resented and feared by the local people. Solicitous of their families at home, Chinese and Indians—and Europeans as well—have sent back many millions of rupees, bhats, and piastres and drained away a large proportion of the foreign exchange surplus that might have been used to develop the Southeast Asian economy. The Chinese, larger in numbers and generally more dramatically successful than the Indians, have naturally aroused the greatest antagonism, though neither race nor religion sharply distinguishes them from the local inhabitants. If the local people admire the Chinese for their diligence, they also envy their worldly success and disapprove of what they consider their noisy manners and dirty personal habits. The unwillingness of either the Nationalist or the Communist government of China to renounce the traditional Chinese rules of citizenship by which children of Chinese men are inalienably Chinese has given even locally born children and grandchildren of Chinese immigrants an ambiguous legal position. Local Chinese have sometimes manipulated the legal ambiguities to their own advantage, claiming Chinese citizenship as a basis for exemption from military duty, for instance, but claiming local citizenship to escape the legal harassments of foreign business firms. At the same time, the possibility of claiming Chinese citizenship has helped to discourage overseas Chinese from identifying themselves with the local people, and has continuously raised among the latter the specter of a potential fifth column. Because of their racial type, the Indians stand out more distinctly from the local people, and they are more likely to differ in religion, but except in Burma, their numbers have been relatively small and their economic successes modest enough to avoid the antagonism aroused by the Chinese. The governments of India and Pakistan have also been far more understanding of the difficulties faced by the newly independent countries and have played less upon the loyalties of their former countrymen than have either of the Chinese governments.

Economic power and political ambiguity have made the immigrant communities one of Southeast Asia's most vexing political problems. Nevertheless, mutual accommodation—or even assimilation—may not be quite such a hopeless prospect as is often believed. Generations of Chinese and Indians have come to Southeast Asia, and their descendants have merged with local population. Only the massive immigration of the first half of this century made the development of permanently distinctive foreign communities a real possibility. Today immigration has been sharply reduced by all Southeast Asian nations and an increasing proportion of the members of the Chinese and Indian communities are locally born, more fluent in the local languages, and more capable of moving naturally among the local people. The division of China has made Chinese nationalism more difficult to maintain and has encouraged local Chinese to cast their lot more decisively with their adopted countries. It is harder now to go back to China for a visit or for an education. Even in Malaya, where the proportion of Chinese is so great that any hope of assimilation is unrealistic, the immigrants have shown an encouraging willingness in the last few years to cooperate with the Malays in building a new nation on the basis of a common Malayan citizenship. Still, both Chinese and Indians retain a love for the land and civilization of their forefathers that is difficult to reconcile with loyalty to their adopted nations.

Chapter Eleven

The Era of Independence

○

World War II: Catalyst for Freedom

In the late 1930's, as Italy and Nazi Germany built their power in Europe, Japan extended her control southward toward Southeast Asia. In 1938, she captured Canton in southern China and early the next year established strategic bases on Hainan and on some of the other islands of the South China Sea. Hong Kong was isolated, and Japanese troops were poised within six hundred miles of Singapore. The Chinese coast was controlled by the Japanese, so that China's only outlets to the world were over land—to Hanoi in Northern French Indo-China or across the mountains to Burma over the newly opened Burma Road. Then, in 1940, France fell to the Germans, and the French colonial government in Indo-China was isolated. Vichy France, under German pressure, granted to Japan the right to use Indo-Chinese bases. In September the Japanese occupied the country as far south as Hanoi; it occupied the remainder the next year. At the same time, Japan courted the Thai government, first by signing a treaty of friendship and later by allowing Thailand to occupy long-coveted parts of Cambodia and Laos. Japan had become a Southeast Asian power.

In December 1941, Japan launched her full-scale attack. Knocking out the American fleet at Pearl Harbor with one arm, she struck southward with the other. Her troops entered Thailand the day after Pearl Harbor, and the Thai government rapidly capitulated and agreed to become an ally of the Japanese. Guam, Wake, and Hong Kong were quickly taken; the Philippines were invaded; and the British navy was crippled in an attempt to protect northern Malaya. One Japanese army moved down through Malaya from the north, another worked westward into Burma, and still others occupied strategic points in Indonesia. Singapore fell in February

1942; Rangoon, in March; and the last American force in the Philippines, in May. Japan had won a stunning victory, and the West had suffered a loss of prestige that even the final defeat of Japan could never restore.

The indigenous people of Southeast Asia played little part in the initial Japanese conquest of their homelands. This was a war between foreign powers—the invaders and the colonial rulers—which the local people had done nothing to bring about and which they were powerless to direct. On the mainland, local troops had rarely been recruited by the colonial powers. Occasionally the local inhabitants assisted and even welcomed the Japanese, but if there was little well-organized support for the defending colonial regimes, neither was there decisive cooperation with the invaders.

Japan should have had an obvious propaganda advantage: as an Asian power, she was demonstrating dramatically that colonial regimes could be overthrown and that Asians could defeat Europeans at their own game. Indeed, Japan did make some attempt to enlist local sympathies. In the Buddhist countries she emphasized the Buddhism they shared, and with considerable fanfare she inaugurated the Japanese "co-prosperity sphere" in which cooperation between the Japanese and Southeast Asians ("Asia for the Asians") was supposed to bring mutual prosperity.

Unfortunately for Japan, however, the behavior of her occupying troops undercut her initial advantages; for the Japanese army must have set a record by its speedy success in antagonizing the local populations. In Singapore, where many Chinese had aided the war effort of their homeland, the Japanese massacred thousands. In Burma, they and some of their new Burmese vassals avenged themselves viciously upon Karen tribesmen, who had supported the British. As for the claim of a common Buddhist tradition, Japanese soldiers acted in ways which to the local people appeared profoundly non-Buddhist: they tramped through holy places in their boots and desecrated pagodas by hanging their dirty clothes upon them. Japanese officers slapped the faces of insubordinate civilians—an indignity no Southeast Asian was likely to forgive.

The conquerors stripped the occupied territories. The European officials and many of their more responsible subordinates had fled or were interned, and local services and distribution of goods ground to a halt. Equipment was looted from hospitals, public health measures collapsed, and malaria, smallpox, cholera, and even bubonic plague broke out and spread. Food from surplus areas could not be shipped to deficit areas and famine resulted. The printing presses turned out ever less valuable money, so that inflation disrupted whatever possibility was left for orderly trade. If the European colonial regimes had been bad, this was far worse, and the inevitable response was a gradually growing resistance to the Japanese.

The jungles of the mountain areas could harbor resistance fighters, just as they had so long sheltered tribesmen from plains rule. Cautiously a few resistance leaders contacted the Allies and obtained weapons to use against the Japanese. Willingness to cooperate with the Allies was always limited however: any movement capable of resisting the Japanese was also capable of resisting the return of Europeans to their prewar position. The seeds of nationalism had flowered. The Japanese were eventually defeated and their troops sent back home, but their years of triumph had shattered forever the appearance of European invincibility. Never again could the nations of Europe assert their former authority. They returned, to be sure, but their days were numbered and with varying degrees of grace they relinquished power to the national governments which now rule.

The New Nations

BURMA. The roots of nationalism actually reach back to the period before the war. As early as 1923, the British had established a legislature in Burma, with a majority of elected members. The legislature was responsible for education, agriculture, public health, and public works, but policies and measures concerning law and order, revenues, and finance remained under direct colonial control. Until 1937 Burma was ruled an integral part of India, but in that year the connection was broken. The Burmese legislature was then reorganized and a ministerial cabinet—patterned after the British government and responsible to the legislature—was created. The British continued to direct foreign relations, defense, and finance, and they retained a special responsibility for the hill areas where the minority tribes lived. Such limited powers could not satisfy the aspirations of nationalist leaders.

In the 1930's Burmese nationalism had found a focus in a student strike at Rangoon University, and the young leader of the strike, Aung San, was later to become the national hero of independent Burma. In 1940 he and a number of other nationalists went to Japan and they returned home with Japan's conquering armies. Aung San became the minister of defense in the new Burmese government organized by the Japanese. Japan intended this government to act as its loyal puppet, but Aung San and his colleagues of the Burma National Army cooperated only as long as they benefited themselves. Under the very noses of the Japanese, they contacted the British forces in India, so that when the Allies moved into Burma, Aung San was ready to lead the Burma National Army out of the Japanese camp and to extend a cautious welcome to the Allies. This sealed the fate of the Japanese in Burma, but at the same time, every British move now had to take into account this new but well-disciplined and well-armed force—an organization which had opposed the Japanese, but which could just as vigorously oppose the return of British rule. The very extent to which the British had cooperated with Aung San and his colleagues during the Japanese occupation made it impossible for them to ignore him after the war, and Aung San would accept nothing short of complete independence.

By 1946 the British acceded to the demands of Aung San's party, the Anti-Fascist Peoples' Freedom League (AFPFL), and gave it a predominant position in the government ratified in the election of April 1947. Britain and the AFPFL seemed to be working toward an orderly transfer of power when, in July, an assassin machine-gunned Aung San and six of his closest cabinet associates as they sat together at a meeting. None of the survivors had the national stature of Aung San, but U Nu, a man previously without such ambitions, became his successor, and independence was granted on schedule in January 1948. Burma was free to run her own affairs.

Almost at once the country was plunged into rebellion. Not one, but two bands of Communist rebels had to be contended with: the so-called "Red Flag" or Trotskyite Communists and the "White Flag" Stalinists. Even more serious were the rebellions fired by minority loyalties. The Karens, a large minority in lower Burma, had often looked with relative favor upon the British and many had become Christians. Many also had suffered horribly during the war, at the hands of the Japanese and of the Burmese as well. They were doubtful about independence and suspicious of Burmese intentions, and in 1949 they rose in revolt. In other parts of the country there were rebellions by the Shans, the Kachins, and an armed insurrection by Chinese Nationalist soldiers who were fleeing from the Communists at home and who lived off the land in Burma. At one time insurgents came within a few miles of Rangoon, but the Burmese army, under the leadership of General Ne Win, slowly pushed them back to the less accessible parts of the country. No problem facing postwar Burma has been more difficult than the position of the non-Burmese minorities. In principle, these minorities were granted considerable autonomy by the Burmese constitution, but their suspicions of the plains people helped to keep the country in continual turmoil.

Until 1958, the AFPFL remained the predominant government party, but in that year it split into two opposing factions, and an even more intense civil war became a real threat. Later that year a military government led by General Ne Win came into power and promptly initiated a number of reforms. It energetically pacified more of the country than at any time since independence and then, to the surprise of many, it supervised elections and turned the government back to the winner, U Nu's faction of the AFPFL. The army had had a taste of power, however, and many observers freely predicted that if civilian rule proved inefficient, indecisive, or at variance with army goals, the army would always be ready to step in again. This happened in 1962, and it appeared that this time the army was prepared to rule for a longer period.

The young Burmese nation had to struggle so desperately to maintain law and order that little energy was left for constructive tasks of development. Many Burmese leaders have had socialist inclinations. Timber lands and some British farms were quickly nationalized, and a state monopoly on rice exports was created. An attempt has been made to establish new industries and start some manufacturing, but it has had only a marginal effect on the economy as a whole. By 1960, exports of rice and timber had not yet reached prewar levels, and Burma remained dependent upon imports for virtually all capital equipment and for many ordinary consumer items as well. In spite of all this, the average Burmese farmer is probably no worse off than he was before the war, simply because the Indian moneylenders who fled the country have not been allowed to return. With the burden of the moneylenders removed, the Burmese farmer has been able to retain a higher proportion of the profits from his crops.

VIETNAM. In French Indo-China, the nationalist movement was led by the Vietnamese. In comparison with their Southeast Asian neighbors, including the Laotians and Cambodians with whom they were grouped under French rule, the Vietnamese are an aggressive people who have absorbed much from the Chinese: technical skills, education, and political doctrines. The Vietnamese also had a relatively large middle class, based upon moneylending, large-scale farming, and the traditional forms of Chinese-style education. These people quickly absorbed the teachings of French nationalism and the French liberal ideology, but they were frustrated by the limitations placed upon their initiative by a paternalistic French administration. The liberal ideas of the West were probably as widely available to the Vietnamese as to any people in Southeast Asia, but the opportunities for putting them into practice were almost nonexistent. In the years between the world wars, the nationalists were so divided among themselves, that no single group could effectively challenge French power. Even then, however, the most single-minded nationalists were the leftwing revolutionaries led by Ho Chi Minh: by 1929 they had formed the core of the new Viet Minh party which was eventually to drive out the French.

The French had done little to stop the Japanese occupation of Indo-China in 1940 and 1941, but the Viet Minh, under the leadership of Ho Chi Minh, organized an active resistance. They received some American weapons and technical aid and they succeeded in clearing the Japanese from several provinces of northern Vietnam. They were thus far more effective in opposing the Japanese than the French government had been. At the end of the war, the French were unable to play a major role in the liberation of Indo-China, but the Allies agreed that the south was to be occupied by British troops, and the north by Chinese, and that the country was then to be turned back to the French authorities. When the Japanese surrendered, however, the Viet Minh was ready to take over Hanoi, and a national committee assumed power in Saigon.

The French showed little willingness to relinquish their former position, but they now had to deal with a well-organized indigenous force, just as the British had in Burma. The French managed to work out agreements with the kings of Laos and Cambodia, granting them a degree of independence, but they faced a more difficult problem in Vietnam. Negotiations became increasingly strained until the positions of the Viet Minh and the French became irreconcilable. The Viet Minh would be satisfied with nothing less than complete independence, while the French government was unwilling to grant more than an advisory function to any local body. In 1946 full-scale war broke out. Perhaps if the Viet Minh had not been Communist-dominated, the French would have been more willing to negotiate with them. Perhaps if the French had granted concessions sooner, the Communists would not have captured what had originally been a predominantly nationalist movement. As it turned out, the dispute that ensued became one of the hottest engagements of the Cold War. The French position became less and less tenable, and although they accepted increasing American aid, the war was long and debilitating. France admitted defeat in 1954, and the Viet Minh inaugurated its period of unchallenged Communist rule in the north.

The "Republic" which was organized in the south first surprised many observers by its viability, but it faced the continual harassment of the Communists. Then, too, the government—using the excuse of a national emergency—brooked so little opposition as to alienate many of the citizens who might have most staunchly resisted the Communists. A military coup in 1963 was followed by another in 1964, and it remained uncertain whether or not popular support could be rallied in time to save the south from Communist domination.

The unrest in South Vietnam has prevented as concentrated an attack upon its economic problems as might have been hoped for. The south has a surplus of rice and a vigorous and hard-working population, but the prosperity which these should create is unlikely until peace is achieved. North Vietnam has followed the example of China in its economic policies: land has been redistributed among the peasants and—with the help of other Communist countries—an attempt has been made to build up industry. Even in the north, however, agricultural production still accounted for 71 per cent of the total national output in 1959, as compared with 82 per cent in 1939.

It appears that the Communists have been far more subtle than the South Vietnamese in their attempt to gain the loyalties of the minorities. The Communists have promised autonomy to the hill people and have promoted their program through cadres whose members speak the local languages and adopt highland ways. The South Vietnamese government, on the other land, has tried to force the mountaineers to settle in permanent villages in the plains and to abandon their traditional way of life, and they have also used the highlands as a settlement area for surplus plains people—none of which is likely to gain sympathy among the hill tribes.

LAOS. No country in the world has had such a confused postwar political history as Laos. Conservatives, moderates, radicals, and Communists have, by turns, jostled for position, formed shifting coalitions, and fought with each other. In spite of massive American aid, no dramatic economic upswing is in sight. The most that can be said for the situation in Laos is that the common man there has never expected much from his government. Because the villagers have always been largely self-sufficient in food and other minimum requirements, the rivalry for power has probably by-passed many of them. The rivalry is, of course, another aspect of the Cold War, and is driven as much by external forces as by internal dissensions, but the internal divisions of a country where as many as half the population are mountaineers have become mixed up with the Cold War issues. The Communist-led Pathet Lao have capitalized upon the resentment of the tribal people toward the lowland Laotians and seem to have gained the support of most of the tribes, and it is the tribes that can supply the best soldiers in the country.

CAMBODIA. Cambodia has been the least unfortunate part of what had been French Indo-China. It had to fight less for the independence that it achieved along with its neighbors. One man, Prince Norodom Sihanouk, has dominated Cambodian politics. Once king of Cambodia; he abdicated in 1955 to assume the premiership and, although he has since jumped in and out of office, his has always been the major voice in the nation. Sihanouk's party has proclaimed socialist goals and a limited start has been made toward industrialization, but the country is still predominantly agricultural. In 1964, it was continuing to walk an uneasy neutralist tightrope, flirting first with the West and then with the Communists.

THAILAND. Thailand has escaped most of the unrest of its neighbors. Avoiding the rigors of a colonial conquest, Thailand managed to modernize its government rapidly enough to maintain independence and flexibility in the changing world. Until 1932, the royal government allowed little scope for initiative outside its ranks, but in that year a coup backed by military officers and by a group of Western-educated Thai succeeded in restricting the powers of the monarchy. The base of governmental control was broadened, but it hardly brought the reality of Western-style democracy to the common people. Since 1932 the country has been ruled by a reasonably benevolent oligarchy, consisting largely of military men.

With its remarkable ability to adjust to the realities of power, Thailand bowed to the inevitable during World War II and became a nominal ally of Japan. Little serious fighting took place in Thailand, though her economy was disrupted and she was treated almost as high-handedly by the Japanese as were the surrounding nations. When peace returned, the leaders who had cooperated with the Japanese were temporarily replaced by others more acceptable to the Allies and the territories annexed from Indo-China were returned. Initial British pressure for war compensation was eventually eased, and Thailand emerged from the war with her monarchy, her territory, and her ruling oligarchy essentially intact.

The Thai have had fewer problems of internal dissension than the countries to the east and west, and they have been reasonably successful in building up their rice production and in encouraging economic expansion. They have also been less suspicious of Western aid and seem to have made relatively good use of it.

Moreover, since the Thai had always taken full responsibility for their own affairs, they may have had fewer unrealistic expectations of a new era. Although the Thai have not had to invest their energies in expelling colonial rulers, similar nationalistic impulses have occasionally been directed against the Chinese who occupy such an important place in the economy. There have been intermittent, but so far only marginally successful, attempts to limit Chinese commercial activity and to expand Thai initiative. With a stronger China now threatening from the north, the Thai have become increasingly suspicious of the intentions of their Chinese minority, though it continues to occupy an essential place in the economy.

THE PERIPHERAL NATIONS. Around the periphery of Southeast Asia independence from the West has also been achieved. Malaya, divided among its mutually suspicious Malay, Chinese, and Indian segments, had some difficulty in developing a common nationalistic sentiment, and for years Communist guerrilla warfare restricted the orderly progress of the country. On the other hand, the wealth of Malaya's rubber and tin has given her the highest per capita income of mainland Asia and has helped to prevent the economic frustration found in so many other countries. A formula for independence was finally worked out which succeeded surprisingly well in preventing the ethnic factions from flying apart. It was as if the dangers of arousing an emotional nationalism in such an ethnically heterogeneous country forced the people and their leaders to deal pragmatically with the problems at hand. The union of Malaya with Singapore and with most of British Borneo in the new nation of Malaysia appeared to be a constructive way of rationalizing the status of these several small states, but the vigorous opposition of Indonesia raised the prospect of still more conflict.

In the north, China came under Communist rule and new roads and regular airplane routes now connect the formerly inaccessible areas near the southern border with the rest of the country. The whole Communist program has been extended to the southern mountains, and their ancient isolation has ended.

As part of India, Assam has shared in the relatively orderly political life of that nation since its independence, but it has presented India with one of its most difficult internal political problems: the relationship of the minority hill peoples to the rest of the nation. Many of the hill peoples have not been satisfied with the constitutional provisions which gave locally elected district councils extensive powers in the semiautonomous hill districts. In some hill areas this dissatisfaction has taken the form of peaceful political agitation for greater local powers, but in the Naga hills on the Burma border the distrust of Indian intentions led some Naga to wage a long and tragic rebellion against India. Certain Naga leaders demanded complete independence, and India responded by sending in its army. To the Indian government the Naga rebellion seemed treasonous, but to many Nagas the Indian response was a new form of colonialism even more threatening than the older forms because it was directed from close by, and backed more powerfully by arms. Some Indians have charged the missionaries, with encouraging separatist ideas, but the causes of distrust between the hill people and the plains-based power of India have far deeper roots.

Conflict: Separatism and Nationalism

Elsewhere in Southeast Asia, the minority people are struggling, sometimes with guns and bullets, sometimes with more peaceful political methods, and sometimes with little except desperate, frustrated anger, for what they feel to be their integrity. Nowhere do they wish to be assimilated into the majority population, for they are proud of their own traditions. No hill man today can escape constant contact with the plains. To the hill peoples, who see men from the plains come into their hills in ever-increasing numbers as tradesmen and professionals, as government bureaucrats and policemen, the threat is a very real one. The plains peoples, on the other hand, always in the majority, forming almost the whole population in parts of each county, may be sadly ignorant of the hills. Those who do not actually travel to the hills may rarely even see a hill man, and they may ignore them until there is a violent rebellion. Like the white Americans who confidently expect the American Indians to assimilate and vanish among the general population, the people of the plains may feel confident that their own civilization is "superior" and destined to submerge more "primitive" ways of life.

Plains people are likely to be far more keenly aware of the other minorities, the immigrant Chinese and Indians—and, in Cambodia, the immigrant Vietnamese. If the hill people fear exploitation by the plains people, so do the latter fear exploitation by the immigrants. The Vietnamese, the Burmese, the Thai, and the Cambodians hold the political power in their countries, and even in Malaya the Malays have so far avoided letting predominant polit-

ical power slip to the Chinese. But everywhere the immigrants occupy so strategic a position in business that their wealth and power
far surpass their numerical proportion of the population.

To these internal conflicts are added, as always, external
pressures. The older form of Western imperialism is gone, but its
memory lingers, as does the fear of Western economic domination
and other, more subtle, kinds of political control. Never before,
even during colonial rule, have outside pressures become so insis-
tent. Political leaders have learned that they may, with reasonable
safety, let loose verbal attacks on the West—sometimes to the en-
hancement of their reputations at home—but Western ideas and
Western technology continue to force their way in. The threat of
the much older form of Chinese imperialism, in its new garb of international Communism, is harder to assess. In the past, Chinese
conquest was rarely a serious threat, but the threat is there today.
The unavoidable presence of China, so large and so near, must act
as a sobering influence on every Southeast Asian political leader.
Unlike England and France, China can never be pushed out to sea
and sent back to another continent.

And so the old themes of Southeast Asian history repeat themselves: the conflict within and the pressure from without. But today,
the threat of force is greater than ever before. Foreign countries
have more power to meddle in the affairs of Southeast Asian
nations, and the national governments have more power to meddle
in the affairs of the minority tribes. The world is no longer the sort
of place in which every small nation can act with unrestricted sover-
eignty or where the hundreds of tribes of Southeast Asia can remain
independent of everyone else. Just as the nations are drawn together
by the airports and bombs provided by modern technology, so the
tribes are forced together by roads and guns. Just as the nations are
unwilling to compromise their hard-won independence to assure international peace, so the tribes are unwilling to abandon their separate interests for the sake of national unity. It is easy to proclaim
that each side must give a little—that the hill people must grant realistically that their future must be bound up with that of the people around them, and that the plains powers must grant to the hill
people the right to their own cultural integrity. To realize such an

ideal is not so simple. The terrain which has so long kept hill man and plainsman apart is no longer a barrier, and it remains for the future to tell whether the diverse people of Southeast Asia will be able to work out the means by which they can live in peace and mutual tolerance, or whether peace will come only with the conquest and assimilation of the proud minorities.

Appendix

The Languages of Southeast Asia

Linguistically, the mainland of Southeast Asia is as confused as any area of the world. Hundreds of distinct languages are spoken and they fall into a half-dozen different families, each of which may be totally unrelated to any of the others. This linguistic diversity poses a grave barrier to unity within the various nations, for the difference in languages tends to perpetuate traditional divisions. The diversity is also a practical problem for the outsider who wishes to study Southeast Asia intensively, as no one can ever master more than an insignificant fraction of the total number of languages. However, language also provides one key by which to gain an understanding of the history and ethnic relationship of the speakers, and so the distribution of the languages and their relationship to one another deserve to be examined.

It is a common observation that, as time passes, all languages gradually change. Even though two communities may start with the same language, they will, unless in constant and intimate contact, gradually diverge in their speech habits. For a while the people of the two communities can be said to speak different dialects, but as their speech grows less similar and as they reach the point at which they can no longer understand each other, they may be said to speak different languages. So long as the similarity of two languages can be recognized, even long after they have ceased to be mutually intelligible, the languages are said to be "genetically related." Genetic relationship shows conclusively that there has been some historical connection between the two, but the exact form of the connection is not always easy to guess. The speakers of one language may have come from the area of the speakers of the other, or both peoples may have come from a third area. The ancestors of one group may have given up their own language and learned their present mode of speech from the ancestors of the other group, or both may have learned their language from a third party. In spite of all these possibilities, it is sometimes possible to make intelligent guesses about the historical contacts between people by investigating the degree of relationship between the languages they speak, for —other things being equal—if two languages are closely related, the ancestors of the two groups must have had relatively recent contact. Great diversity among related languages may be an indication of long settlement, while relative homogeneity is likely to mean that a language group has spread so recently that its members have not had time to become distinct.

As centuries and millennia pass, a time will come (after perhaps five thousand years or so) when two languages grow so different that it is difficult or impossible to say whether or not they are related. Thus linguists recognize a number of separate language families over the world which, so far as anyone can tell, are completely unrelated to each other. However, the criteria for determining whether or not two dissimilar groups of languages are distantly related are sometimes difficult to apply, and scholars often differ radically in their judgments. For this reason it is often impossible to state categorically which languages are definitely related and which are not. This would be a matter of interest only to linguistic scholars, except that an interpretation of the movements of the languages and of the people who spoke them may rest upon this imperfect judgment.

For these reasons, any list of languages and of their genetic relationships must be accepted with considerable caution. In the list given on the following pages, the various languages are divided among eight families. Most people who have dealt with Southeast Asian languages would probably consider all of the languages listed under the same family to be related. Comments suggesting the wider relationships among the families that various scholars have proposed are given in italics. At one time or another every group has been thought to be related to one or more of the others, but none of the theories of wider relationships is universally accepted. The various suggestions are shown in this manner in the hope that the reader will realize the uncertainty of the relationships, and sense the spirit of doubt and disagreement which divides the experts.

The goal of linguistic classification is not only to decide whether or not two languages are related, but also to group together those languages of the same family which have been separated from each other for a relatively short time into subgroups and subsubgroups. This also is often a difficult task, but a guess about subgrouping is given for a number of the families on the list.

Language Families of Southeast Asia

1. MIAO-YAO. Yao is spoken in southern China (Kwangsi and Yunnan), in northernmost Vietnam, in the Laotian hills, and in northern Thailand. Yao is sometimes called Man, though the latter term is also used to refer to any southern Chinese aboriginal. Miao (or Meo) is concentrated in Kweichow, but also spoken in Yuannan, Szechwan, Kwangsi, Laos, northern Vietnam, and northern Thailand, usually in the high hills.

Miao-Yao is often considered to be a branch of Sino-Tibetan along with Tibeto-Burmese, but it has sometimes been thought to be related to Mon-Khmer.

2. TIBETO-BURMESE. Tibeto-Burmese is usually thought to be related to Chinese (forming the Sino-Tibetan family), though a few linguists are skeptical of this relationship. Sapir and a few others have suggested that Sino-Tibetan (including Tibeto-Burmese) may be further related to the Athebascan languages of North America, but no satisfactory evidence for this has ever been presented.

Besides the Southeast Asian subgroups listed here, Tibeto-Burmese includes Tibetan and a large number of languages of the southern fringes of the Himalayas in southern Tibet, Nepal, and northernmost India.

A. BODO, etc. Garo, Kachari, and Koch of western Assam are closely related to each other and possibly slightly less closely related to Chutua and Lalung of the upper Assam valley and to Tipera just south of Assam. Somewhat more remotely related are Konyak and a few other languages of the eastern-most Naga hills. Jinghpaw, spoken in northern Burma, may be a rather distant member of the same subgroup.

B. KUKI-CHIN, etc. Lushai, the various Kuki languages spoken in and near Manipur, and the Chin languages of western Burma form a closely related subgroup. Several other languages are probably somewhat more divergent members of the same subgroup: Manipuri (also known as Meithei); Lhota, Ao, and some others of the Naga hills; and Mikir.

C. NAGA. The remaining languages of the Naga hills seem to form another subgroup. Angami, Sema, and Rengma show clear similarities to one another, while Thankul and some others may be more divergent members of the same subgroup.

D. BURMESE-LOLO. This branch falls quite clearly into two subbranches, which still show significant similarities with one another. The Lolo group includes Lolo itself in Yunnan, western Szechwan, and Vietnam; Akha (or Kaw) in Thailand, Laos, the eastern Burmese Shan states, and southern China; and Lisu and Lahu in north Burma. The Burma group includes Burmese itself and the so-called Kachin languages of northern Burma (Maru, Atzi, Lashi, and others) except for Jinghpaw. Jinghpaw, often confusingly called "Kachin proper" is linguistically very different.

E. KAREN. This branch includes numerous languages spoken in southern Burma, both in the plains, and in the hills along the Thai border. Karen includes at least two main subbranches, one of which includes Pwo, and the other, Sgaw, but there are many other Karen languages which may fall into either of these subbranches, or into entirely different ones.[1] It is occasionally doubted whether Karen is Tibeto-Burmese at all, but its similarities to other Tibeto-Burmese languages are so great that continued doubt seems unreasonable.

F. NORTH BURMA. Nung and Rawang spoken in northernmost Burma, do not seem closely related to any of the groups listed above, although it has been claimed that they are similar to Tibetan.

G. NORTH ASSAM. Abor, Miri, Dafla, and Mishmi of the Himalayan slopes of northern Assam form a rather homogeneous subgroup. As in the case of the North Burma branch, it has been claimed that they have a special resemblance to Tibetan, but they show no obvious similarity to the North Burma group.

H. KADU-KANANG-SAK-THET-ANDRO. These obscure languages are very little known and are spoken only in a few isolated spots along the Burma-Assam border, in Manipur, and in Chitagong, East Pakistan. It has been claimed that these form a separate subgroup.

Traditionally Thai has been considered related to Chinese and hence to Tibeto-Burmese. Most linguists now feel this to be an unjustified belief, which was made possible only by extensive Thai borrowings from Chinese, which have given Thai a superficial resemblance to that language.

3. THAI.[2]

A. Siamese, Laotian, Shan of Burma, Ahom of Assam, Lu of South China, and Black Thai and White Thai of North Vietnam.

B. Several languages of the border region between North Vietnam and Kwangsi: Tay, Tho, Nung, Lungchow, Tien-pao, Yung-chun.

C. Several languages, mostly in Kwangsi to the north of Subgroup B: Wu-ming, Chien-chiang, Tse-heng, Ling-yun, Hsi-lin, Tien-chow, Po-ai.

Henri Maspero published evidence attempting to prove that Thai and Vietnamese are related.[3]

4. VIETNAMESE-MUONG. Muong is spoken in the highlands to the southwest of the Red River delta of northern Vietnam.

Schmidt related Vietnamese and Mon-Khmer and also the Munda languages of central India into his "Austro-Asiatic group."[4] J. Greenberg accepts this but many linguists remain skeptical.[5]

5. MON-KHMER. The following divisions are made along geographical and traditional lines because not enough work has been done on most of these languages to allow a reliable genetic classification. A few linguists remain doubtful about the relation of some of the divisions (particularly Groups E, F, and G) to Mon and Khmer, the two most important members of the family.

A. MON. The language of the early kingdoms in southern Burma, and still spoken by a minority of people there.

B. KHMER. The language of the Cambodians.

C. PALAUNG-WA. Lawa and Chaobon are spoken in Thailand, Palaung and Wa in the northwest Shan states of Burma.

D. SOUTHEASTERN. The languages of most of the so-called *Moi* tribes of Vietnam and Laos, and of similar tribes, generically termed *Pnong* in Cambodia and *Kha* in Thailand.

E. SEMANG and SAKAI, spoken in the interior of the Malay Peninsula by Negritos and other aboriginal tribes.

F. NICOBARESE, spoken in the Nicobar Islands.

G. KHASI, spoken to the south of the Brahamaputra River in Assam.

Schmidt further related his "Austro-Asiatic" group (Munda, Mon-Khmer, and Vietnamese) with Malayo-Polynesian, into a still larger family which he called "Austric." [6] Most linguists are skeptical of this.

6. MALAYO-POLYNESIAN. Except for Malay, the language of the Malay peninsula, the only Malayo-Polynesian languages spoken on the mainland are Cham and a few hill languages such as Rhade and Jarai, all of which are found in southern Vietnam. Other Malayo-Polynesian languages stretch from Madagascar to Hawaii and include the many languages of both Indonesia and the Philippines.

Paul Benedict has offered evidence to show that the Kadai languages are related both to Thai and to Malayo-Polynesian, and hence that all three groups are related. Linguists seem to be divided in their opinions about this suggestion.

7. KADAI. Benedict suggested that several obscure languages (Li of Hainan off the southern China coast; Laqua and Lati in northernmost Vietnam;

and Kelao of Kweichow and northern Vietnam) are all related to each other.[7]

8. ANDAMANESE. Until recently, no one had suggested that Andamanese was related to any other language anywhere, but Greenberg has now suggested that it may be related to the languages of Australia and to those of the Papua in New Guinea.

The Spread of the Languages

To the extent that this classification is reliable, a few guesses can be made about the history of the spread of the languages. As has been emphasized earlier in this book, the spread of a language need not require a complete population displacement, because people sometimes shift from one language to another, but languages do not spread chaotically, and if one language displaces another, it is generally for some clear reason—the cultural, political, or technical dominance of its speakers, if not their actual migration and conquest. For this reason, inferences about the spread of languages have a bearing upon the spread of other cultural phenomena.

The lonely position of Andamanese inevitably suggests that it has been very anciently established on its islands. Even if Andamanese should eventually prove to be related to the languages of Australia and Papua, it is difficult to imagine that the ancestors of the Andamanese could have brought their language from the east in any recent time without leaving some trace in between. At the very least, it seems that Andamanese must have been isolated for many centuries. The Mon-Khmer languages are scattered into rather isolated pockets strewn about the whole of the Southeast Asian mainland. Such a distribution could have come about if the contact among a group of languages which had once been spread rather continuously was broken by the arrival of other languages. If Vietnamese is related to Mon-Khmer, the picture is not altered substantially, and even if the Munda language of India should prove to be related to both, it still looks as though this group of languages is very anciently established.

The major Thai languages form a closely homogeneous group stretching from Assam to Laos. It cannot have been many centuries since these languages (or dialects) first started to diverge from one another. There is more diversity among the obscure but related languages of the Vietnam-China border, and it is difficult to avoid the conclusion that this was the center from which the Thai languages spread. If Thai is related to Kadai, this makes such a supposition even more likely, because the Kadai languages are also found in the same general area.

Malayo-Polynesian is represented on the mainland only by a few languages of southern Vietnam, and by the language of the Malays. It has been variously thought to be related either to Mon-Khmer or to Thai-Kadai, and both these suggestions have been used to support the idea that the Malayo-Polynesian languages originally spread from the mainland. There is, however, evidence within the Malayo-Polynesian family which suggests that their greatest diversity—and hence perhaps the center from which they spread—is to be found much farther east, somewhere in Melanesia. It is possible that the mainland languages of this family were originally brought by settlers traveling westward out of the islands, rather than the other way round. This would not exclude the possibility that at a very remote time the ancestor of the Malayo-Polynesian languages may have come from the mainland, but it seems increasingly likely that only after reaching Melanesia did the ancestors of the present subdivisions split up and spread in all directions.

The Tibeto-Burmese languages are concentrated in the western and northern parts of Southeast Asia and have often been attributed to rather late migration from the north. These languages are far more diverse than the major Thai languages, however, and this suggests that the Tibeto-Burmese subdivisions have been separated for much longer. Certainly Tibeto-Burmese languages have been spoken in most of their present area for as long as there are records, although southern Burma—where Burmese has largely displaced Mon—is an exception. Assam, where Indo-European Assamese replaced what appears to have been an earlier Tibeto-Burmese language, looks like an area where this language family has actually retreated. If we accept the usual but not universal belief that Chinese is related to the Tibeto-Burmese languages (in a larger Sino-Tibetan group), than either Chinese spread northward or the Tibeto-Burmese languages spread southward. The historical importance of the Chinese, together with the historical knowledge that the earliest

Chinese civilization grew up in northern China has led many people to conclude that the Tibeto-Burmese languages must have moved southward. However, the far greater diversity of the Tibeto-Burmese languages would argue for a long history of splitting, and they may have been in their present area for a very long time.

Because language has often become the prime symbol of group identity for the people of Southeast Asia, difficulties arise for anyone who would try to infer history from language distribution. When people have wanted to assert their individuality, they have, like the Irish and Israelis, seized upon a unique language and made it the sign of their separation. In the course of the centuries, as political fortunes and popular aspirations have waxed and waned, people seem to have repeatedly shifted their language affiliation in defiance of stability or historical purity. The complex distribution of languages must be understood partly in these terms. Because the historical pressures in the plains have been toward unity and homogeneity, the plains areas have relatively few and widespread languages. Because the historical pressures in the hills have encouraged separatism, the hills harbor most of the many hundreds of Southeast Asian languages. It is worth pointing out, however, that almost every language family includes both a number of languages spoken in the hills and another which is spoken (and written) on the plains. Whatever the history of the spread and distribution of languages, it has little to do with the contrast between hills and plains that is so important for so many other facets of Southeast Asian life.

The contrast between life in the hills and in the plains does show up in one linguistic characteristic: languages spoken in the plains often have complex ways of indicating the social position of the speaker relative to the person he is addressing. One often has to choose carefully from several pronouns corresponding to *I*, depending upon whether one is addressing a member of the royalty, a holy man, a social superior, an equal, or a servant. Languages spoken in the more fluid social system of the hills are less likely to force such distinctions.

Almost all the languages of Southeast Asia are characterized by the use of a grammatical device known as *numeral classifiers*. Whenever a number is used, it must be associated with a special marker (classifier) which somehow indicates the sort of thing being

counted. Furthermore, most of the languages belonging to the Tibeto-Burmese, Thai, Vietnamese, and Miao-Yao groups (though apparently not those of the Mon-Khmer or Malayo-Polynesian families) are characterized by distinctive tones, so that two words pro-
nounced in the same way except for a difference in the pitch or tone
may still be entirely distinct in meaning and use.

Southeast Asian languages, particularly those spoken in the hills,
have often been accused of lacking words for abstract concepts, and
it has even been suggested that the speakers are so limited by their
vocabulary as to be incapable of abstract thought. Such a suggestion
is nonsense, and belief in the deficiency of abstract terms can only
be held by one who has not learned such a language very well or by
one who has preconceived ideas about the superiority of his own
speech. Each of these hundreds of languages is, in fact, a complex
and flexible medium, capable of being applied to all the same uses
as any other language.

The typological resemblances among many of these languages,
and the fact that one scholar or another has felt it reasonable to suggest that so many of them are related in one way or another, might
raise one final possibility. Could it be that *all* these languages are,
even if only very remotely, related to each other in one great super-
family? Such a hypothesis should probably not be dismissed completely, though it seems more likely that the similarities can be explained by mutual borrowing throughout the long course of the history of these languages. These languages have long been in close
contact, and there has been mass bilingualism. In such circumstances, the characteristics of neighboring languages—their vocabu-
laries, pronunciation, and even grammar—may affect each other. As
a result, languages can come to resemble each other in many ways,
even though they go back to different antecedents.

Notes

1. R. B. Jones, *Karen Linguistic Studies*. University of California Publications in
   Linguistics, Vol. 25 (Berkeley: University of California Press, 1961).
2. Fang-Kuei Li, "Classification by Vocabulary: Tai Dialects," *Anthropological
   Linguistics*, I (1959), 15-21.
3. H. Maspero, "Études sur la phonétique historique de la langue annamite,"
   Bulletin de l'École française d'extrême-Orient, XII (1912).
4. Wilhelm Schmidt, *Die Mon-Khmer Völker* (Braunschweig: F. Vieweg & Sohn,
   1906).

5. Joseph Greenberg, "Historical Linguistics and Unwritten Languages," in A. L. Kroeber (ed.), *Anthropology Today* (Chicago: University of Chicago Press, 1953).
6. Wilhelm Schmidt, *Die Gliederung der Australischen Sprachen* (Vienna: Mechitharsten-Buchdrückerei, 1919).
7. Paul Benedict, "Thai, Kadai, and Indonesian, a New Alignment in Southeast Asia," *American Anthropologist*, XLIV (1942), 576-601.

Selected Bibliography

The works listed here include only those which I have found most valuable and which can be recommended to others. Further bibliographic guidance may be obtained from *Southeast Asian History: A Bibliographic Guide* by Stephen N. Hay and Margaret H. Case (New York: Frederick A. Praeger, 1962), which is unusually well annotated, though it is weighted on the side of history and modern political developments and is limited in its ethnographic coverage. A massive, but less up-to-date anthropological bibliography of Southeast Asia is *Bibliography of the Peoples and Cultures of Mainland Southeast Asia* by John F. Embree and Lillian Ota Dotson (New Haven: Yale University Southeast Asian Studies, 1950). Each year the *Journal of Asian Studies* publishes a bibliography as Number 5 of its volume for the year. This is the most essential tool for current bibliography of Southeast Asia as well as for other parts of the continent.

General

Dobby, E. H. G. *Southeast Asia.* London: University of London Press, 1950. A standard treatment of Southeast Asian geography, land forms, natural resources, industrial production, and so on.

Dubois, Cora. *Social Forces in Southeast Asia.* Cambridge, Mass.: Harvard University Press, 1959. A sensitive interpretation of the factors bringing change to Southeast Asian society in the postwar years.

Heine-Geldern, Robert. "'Südostasian," in G. Buschan (ed.), *Illustrierte Völkerkunde.* Stuttgart: 1923. A standard and much cited synthesis of Southeast Asian ethnology, but rather outdated in its manner of interpretation.

————. *Conception of State and Kingship in Southeast Asia,* Cornell University Southeast Asia Program, Data papers No. 18. Ithaca, N.Y., 1956.

Landon, Kenneth P. *Southeast Asia, Crossroad of Religions.* Chicago: University of Chicago Press, 1949. A somewhat scattered account by a missionary who tries, without complete success, to be fair to religions other than his own.

LeBar, Frank, Gerald C. Hicky, and John K. Musgrave. *Ethnic Groups of Mainland Southeast Asia*. New Haven: Human Relations Areas Files Press, 1964.

Prehistory

Colani, Madeleine. *L'âge de la pierre dans la province de Hoa-binh*. Hanoi: Mémoires du Service Géologique de l'Indochine, 1927. Vol. XIV. fasc. 1.

Mansuy, Henri. *Contribution à l'étude de la préhistoire de l'Indochine*, Parts 1-8. Hanoi: Bulletin du Service Géologique de l'Indochine and Mémoires du Service Géologique de l'Indochine, 1920–25. Vol. 7–14.

Movius, Hallam L., Jr. *Early Man and Pleistocene Stratigraphy in Southern and Eastern Asia*. Papers of the Peabody Museum of American Archeology and Ethnology, 19. Cambridge, Mass., 1944. (The works by Colani, Mansuy and Movius are technical accounts of archaeological investigations.)

Sauer, Carl. *Agricultural Origins and Dispersals*. New York: American Geographical Society, 1952. An attempt to fix the history of cultivated crops throughout the world.

Tweedie, M. W. F. *Prehistoric Malaya*. Singapore: Donald Moor, 1957. A short, comparatively readable survey of Malayan prehistory.

*History**

Coedès, G. *Les États hindouisés d'Indochine et d'Indonésie*. Paris: E. de Boccard, 1948. A ground-breaking synthesis of knowledge of the early historical period.

Hall, D. G. E. *A History of Southeast Asia*. London: Macmillan & Co., Ltd., 1961. A formidable collection of facts, weighted toward the colonial period.

Harrison, Brian. *Southeast Asia: A Short History*. London: Macmillan & Co., Ltd., 1960. The only brief and readable history of Southeast Asia.

Hill People

Burling, Robbins. *Rengsanggri: Family and kinship in a Garo village*. Philadelphia: University of Pennsylvania Press, 1963.

Condominas, George. *Nous Avons Mangé La Forêt*. Paris: Mercure de France, 1957. A chronicle of life among a hill tribe in South Vietnam.

Evans, Ivor Hugh Norman. *The Negritos of Malaya*. Cambridge: Cambridge University Press, 1937. The most accessible and general of

* Besides the general works listed here, note the sources given in the footnotes to Chapter 5.

several books on Malayan aborigines, but somewhat old-fashioned in approach.

Hutton, John H. *The Angami Nagas.* London: Macmillan & Co., Ltd., 1921. One of the better traditional ethnographies by a British official.

Izikowitz, K. G. *Lamet: Hill Peasants in French Indo-China. Etnografiska Studier* No. 17. Goteborg: Etnografiska Museet, 1951. A solid and general description of a tribe in Laos.

Leach, E. R. *Political Systems of Highland Burma.* Cambridge, Mass.: Harvard University Press, 1954. A technical and theoretical account of shifting power relationships.

Mills, James P. *The Ao Nagas.* London: Macmillan & Co., Ltd., 1926. A standard ethnography by a British official.

Radcliffe-Brown, A. R. *The Andaman Islanders.* Cambridge: Cambridge University Press, 1922. An aging anthropological classic.

Stevenson, H. N. C. *The Economics of the Central Chin Tribes.* Bombay: Times of India Press, 1943. A rather specialized, but solid treatment.

Burma

Brant, Charles S. *Tadagale: A Burmese Village in 1950.* Cornell University Southeast Asia Program, Data Papers No. 13. Ithaca, N.Y., 1954. A short description.

Cady, John F. *A History of Modern Burma.* Ithaca, N.Y.: Cornell University Press, 1958. A tedious but voluminous account of colonial and post-colonial political history.

Mi Mi Khaing. *Burmese Family.* Calcutta: Longmans, Green & Company, Ltd., 1946. Bloomington, Ind.: Indiana University Press, 1962. A Burman's warm reminiscences of her girlhood.

Shway, Yoe (pseudonym of Sir James George Scott). *The Burman: His Life and Notions.* London: Macmillan & Co., Ltd., 1910. New York: W. W. Norton & Company, Inc., 1963. An old but delightful account of all things Burmese by a remarkable Briton.

Thailand

Benedict, Ruth. *Thai Culture and Behavior.* Cornell University Southeast Asia Program, Data Paper No. 4. Ithaca, N.Y., 1952. An interpretation by a sensitive anthropologist who, however, never visited Thailand.

deYoung, John E. *Village Life in Modern Thailand.* Berkeley and Los Angeles: University of California Press, 1955. A readable and straightforward account of village life.

Kaufman, Howard Keva. *Bangkhuad: A Community Study in Thailand.*

Locust Valley, N.Y.: Published for the Association for Asian Studies by Augustin (Monographs of the Association for Asian Studies, 10), 1960.

Kingshill, Konrad. *Ku Daeng, the Red Tomb: A Village Study in Northern Thailand.* Chiangmai: Prince Royal's College, 1960.

Vietnam, Laos, and Cambodia

Briggs, Lawrence Palmer. *The Ancient Khmer Empire.* Transactions of the American Philosophical Society, 1951. A standard history.

Cadière, Léopold. *Croyances et pratiques religieuses des Viêtnamiens.* Paris: École Française d'Extrême-Orient, Vol. I, 1944; Vol. II, 1955; Vol. III, 1957. Massive and detailed descriptions of many aspects of Vietnamese religious life.

Delvert, Jean. *Le Paysan Cambodigien.* The Hague: Mouton, 1961. The work of a geographer who concentrates on climate, land use, agriculture, and economy.

Gourou, Pierre. *Peasants of the Tonkin Delta, a Story of Human Geography,* translated by Richard R. Millar. New Haven: Human Relations Area Files, 1955. Another work by a geographer, and a standard source.

Langrant, Gustave. *Vie Sociale et Religieuse en Annam, monographe d'un village de la côte Sud Annam.* Lille: Univers, 1945. A study of a fishing village.

LeBar, Frank, and Adrienne Suddard (eds.). *Laos: Its People, Its Society, Its Culture.* New Haven: Human Relations Area Files, 1960. The only available work which attempts to bring data of Laos together in one place.

Robequain, Charles. *Le Thanh Hoá: Étude Géographique d'une Province Annamite.* 2 vols. Paris and Bruxelles: Les Éditions G. Van Oest, 1929.

Southeast Asian Chinese

Freedman, Maurice. *Chinese Family and Marriage in Singapore.* Colonial Research Studies, No. 20. London: H. M. Stationery Office, 1957.

Purcell, Victor. *The Chinese in Southeast Asia.* Royal Institute of International Affairs and the Institute of Pacific Relations. London, New York: G. Cumberlege, Oxford University Press, Inc., 1951.

Skinner, George William. *Chinese Society in Thailand: An Analytical History.* Ithaca, New York: Cornell University Press, 1957. This and the following work by Skinner are outstanding and detailed studies.

———. *Leadership and Power in the Chinese Community of Thailand.* Ithaca, N.Y.: Published for the Association for Asian Studies by Cornell University Press, 1958. (Monographs of the Association for Asian Studies, 3.)

Southeast Asia in the Modern World

Bone, Robert C. *Contemporary Southeast Asia.* New York; Random House, 1962.

Butwell, Richard. *Southeast Asia Today and Tomorrow: A Political Analysis.* New York: Frederick A. Praeger, Inc., 1961.

Kahin, George McT. (ed.). *Governments and Politics of Southeast Asia.* Ithaca, N.Y.: Cornell University Press, 1959.

Vandenbosch, Amry, and Richard Butwell. *Southeast Asia Among the World Powers.* Lexington: University of Kentucky Press, 1957.

INDIA, CEYLON and the WEST	BURMA — Upper	BURMA — Lower	THAILAND	MALAYA	CAMBODIA	CHAMPA	VIETNAM	CHINA
-100 A.D.					Funan flourishes from early Christian centuries until its fall about 550 A.D.	Linyi	North Vietnam controlled by China until	Han Dynasty 202 B.C. to 220 A.D.
Buddhism flourishes in Ceylon, 5th Century.	Pyus in upper Burma	Mons in Mekong and lower Burma						
600							939	T'ang Dynasty 618 to 907
	Pagan founded ca. 849	Mons in lower Burma			Angkor, under the Khmer, rises and flourishes, 9th to 12th Centuries.	Champa flourishes.	Vietnamese press southward against Chams.	Sung Dynasty 960 to 1279
	King Anawrata (1044–1077) unites Burma.							
1200		Pagan falls to Mongols, 1287	Thai expand following Mongols					Yüan (Mongol) Dynasty 1260 to 1368
Muslims well established in India by 14th Century		Mons independent in lower Burma	Thai rule from Ayutthaya.			Champa increasingly pressed by Vietnamese		Ming Dynasty 1368 to 1644
1400								

INDIA, CEYLON and the WEST	BURMA Upper	BURMA Lower	THAILAND	MALAYA	CAMBODIA	CHAMPA	VIETNAM	CHINA
—1400								
Portuguese in India	Burma reunited under Toungoo Dynasty			Malacca flourishes under Muslim rulers.	Angkor abandoned, 1460			
				Portuguese take Malacca, 1511.				
—1600								
British begin conquest of India.	Alaungpaya Dynasty from 1756	Thai-Burmese wars, Ayutthaya sacked, 1765. Bangkok founded.		Dutch take Malacca, 1641.			Chams virtually absorbed by Vietnamese	Manchu Dynasty 1644 to 1912
—1800								
Industrial Revolution brings new colonialism.	British take Burma in three Burmese wars.			British power consolidated in Malaya	French take "Indo-china"			
—1900								

Japanese conquest and reassertion of independence.

Index

Some Related ⓐ Spectrum Books

Understanding Other Cultures, *Dorothy Lee*, S-6

The First Russian Revolution: Its Impact on Asia, *Ivar Spector*, S-27

Communist China's Strategy in the Nuclear Era, *Alice Langley Hsieh*, S-32

Man's Discovery of His Past, *edited by Robert F. Heizer*, S-46

Understanding Other Cultures, *Ina Corinne Brown*, S-49

A Guide to the World's Religions, *David G. Bradley*, S-51

The Realities of World Communism, *edited by William Petersen*, S-60

History and Future of Religious Thought: Christianity, Hinduism, Buddhism, Islam, *Philip H. Ashby*, S-64

Triumph in the Pacific: The Navy's Struggle Against Japan, *edited by E. B. Potter and Chester W. Nimitz*, S-66

World Pressures on American Foreign Policy, *edited by Marian D. Irish*, S-80

Politics of the Developing Nations, *Fred R. von der Mehden*, S-88

Man Before History, *edited by Creighton Gabel* (Global History series), S-92

Traditional India, *edited by O. L. Chavarria-Aguilar* (Asian Civilization series), S-100

Modern China, *edited by Albert Feuerwerker* (Asian Civilization series), S-101

Self-Government in Modernizing Nations, *edited by J. Roland Pennock*, S-107

The Cold War . . . and After, *Charles O. Lerche, Jr.*, S-117

The United States and the Far East (Second Edition), *edited by Willard L. Thorp* (American Assembly series), S-AA-6